Do The Math® NOW!

Multiplication & Division

WorkSpace

Cover: © Jacques Alexandre/age fotostock
No part of this publication may be reproduced in whole or in part, or stored in a retrieval system, or transmitted in any form or by any means, electronic, mechanical, photocopying, recording, or otherwise, without written permission of the publisher. For information regarding permission, write to Scholastic Inc., 557 Broadway, New York, NY 10012.

ISBN-13: 978-0-545-39439-0
ISBN-10: 0-545-39439-2

4   5   6   7   8   9   10   40   20   19   18   17   16   15   14   13

Table of Contents

Multiplication Chart

X	1	2	3	4	5	6	7	8	9	10	11	12
1	1	2	3	4	5	6	7	8	9	10	11	12
2	2	4	6	8	10	12	14	16	18	20	22	24
3	3	6	9	12	15	18	21	24	27	30	33	36
4	4	8	12	16	20	24	28	32	36	40	44	48
5	5	10	15	20	25	30	35	40	45	50	55	60
6	6	12	18	24	30	36	42	48	54	60	66	72
7	7	14	21	28	35	42	49	56	63	70	77	84
8	8	16	24	32	40	48	56	64	72	80	88	96
9	9	18	27	36	45	54	63	72	81	90	99	108
10	10	20	30	40	50	60	70	80	90	100	110	120
11	11	22	33	44	55	66	77	88	99	110	121	132
12	12	24	36	48	60	72	84	96	108	120	132	144

Things That Come in Groups

DIRECTIONS

➤ Write more things on the lists.

Groups of 2
slices of bread in a sandwich
twins
wheels on a bicycle
socks

Groups of 3
legs on a stool
wheels on a scooter
sides on a triangle
feet in a yard

Things That Come in Groups

DIRECTIONS

➤ Write more things on the lists.

Groups of 4
wheels on a car
wheels on a skateboard
sides on a square

Groups of 5
fingers on a hand
points on a star

Groups of 6	
legs on an insect	
strings on a guitar	

Equal Groups Problems

1

There are 5 bikes.

Each has 2 wheels.

How many wheels are there in all?

Read the word problem.

2

$5 \times 2 = \boxed{}$

Write the multiplication equation.

3

2, 4, 6, 8, 10

Show your figuring.

4

$5 \times 2 = \boxed{10}$

Write the answer.

1

EQUATION

WORD PROBLEM

There are 6 sandwiches.

Each has 2 slices of bread.

How many slices of bread are there in all?

FIGURING

2

EQUATION

WORD PROBLEM

There are 5 ants.

Each has 6 legs.

How many legs are there in all?

FIGURING

Equal Groups Problems

DIRECTIONS

1
There are 5 bikes.

Each has 2 wheels.

How many wheels are there in all?

Read the word problem.

2
$5 \times 2 = \boxed{}$

Write the multiplication equation.

3
2, 4, 6, 8, 10

Show your figuring.

4
$5 \times 2 = \boxed{10}$

Write the answer.

① EQUATION

WORD PROBLEM

There are 5 pickup trucks.

Each has 4 wheels.

How many wheels are there in all?

FIGURING

② EQUATION

WORD PROBLEM

There are 6 dogs.

Each has 4 legs.

How many legs are there in all?

FIGURING

Multiplication Word Problems

DIRECTIONS

1

$3 \times 2 = \boxed{}$

Look at the multiplication equation.

2

There are 3 bikes .

Each has 2 wheels .

How many wheels are there in all?

Write a word problem.

3

2, 4, 6

Show your figuring.

4

$3 \times 2 = \boxed{6}$

Write the answer in the box.

---

1 **EQUATION**

$2 \times 6 = \boxed{}$

WORD PROBLEM

There are _____.

Each has _____.

How many _____ are there in all?

FIGURING

2 **EQUATION**

$5 \times 4 = \boxed{}$

WORD PROBLEM

There are _____.

Each has _____.

How many _____ are there in all?

FIGURING

Multiplication Word Problems

DIRECTIONS

➤ Look at the multiplication equation.
➤ Write a word problem.
➤ Show your figuring.
➤ Write the answer in the box.

1

EQUATION

$6 \times 4 = \boxed{}$

WORD PROBLEM

There are _____.

Each has _____.

How many _____ are there in all?

FIGURING

2

EQUATION

$5 \times 5 = \boxed{}$

WORD PROBLEM

There are _____.

Each has _____.

How many _____ are there in all?

FIGURING

Multiplication Word Problems

> DIRECTIONS

- ➤ Look at the multiplication equation.
- ➤ Write a word problem.
- ➤ Show your figuring.
- ➤ Write the answer in the box.

①

EQUATION

$3 \times 4 = \boxed{}$

WORD PROBLEM

There are _____.

Each has _____.

How many _____ are there in all?

FIGURING

②

EQUATION

$4 \times 3 = \boxed{}$

WORD PROBLEM

There are _____.

Each has _____.

How many _____ are there in all?

FIGURING

More Multiplication Word Problems

➤ Look at the multiplication equation.
➤ Write a word problem.
➤ Show your figuring.
➤ Write the answer in the box.

1 EQUATION

6 × 6 = ☐

WORD PROBLEM

There are _____.

Each has _____.

How many _____ are there in all?

FIGURING

2 EQUATION

4 × 6 = ☐

WORD PROBLEM

There are _____.

Each has _____.

How many _____ are there in all?

FIGURING

Show What You Know

DIRECTIONS

➤ Look at the multiplication equation.
➤ Write a word problem.
➤ Show your figuring.
➤ Write the answer in the box.

1 EQUATION

$4 \times 4 = \boxed{}$

WORD PROBLEM

There are _____.

Each has _____.

How many _____

are there in all?

FIGURING

2 EQUATION

$6 \times 3 = \boxed{}$

WORD PROBLEM

There are _____.

Each has _____.

How many _____

are there in all?

FIGURING

3 EQUATION

$5 \times 3 = \boxed{}$

WORD PROBLEM

There are _____.

Each has _____.

How many _____

are there in all?

FIGURING

Show What You Know

DIRECTIONS

> ➤ Look at the multiplication equation.
> ➤ Write a word problem.
> ➤ Show your figuring.
> ➤ Write the answer in the box.

1 EQUATION

$6 \times 5 = \boxed{}$

WORD PROBLEM

There are _____.

Each has _____.

How many _____

are there in all?

FIGURING

2 EQUATION

$5 \times 6 = \boxed{}$

WORD PROBLEM

There are _____.

Each has _____.

How many _____

are there in all?

FIGURING

3 EQUATION

$4 \times 2 = \boxed{}$

WORD PROBLEM

There are _____.

Each has _____.

How many _____

are there in all?

FIGURING

Game Rules for Circles and Stars Capture

HOW TO PLAY

What you need

- *Circles and Stars Capture* cards, 9 cards per player
- *WorkSpace* pages 14 and 15

➤ **Each turn has three steps.**

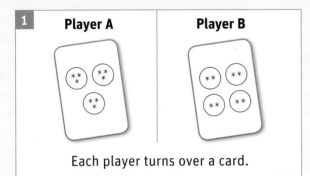

1

| Player A | Player B |

Each player turns over a card.

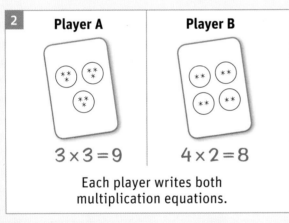

2

| Player A | Player B |

$3 \times 3 = 9$ $4 \times 2 = 8$

Each player writes both
multiplication equations.

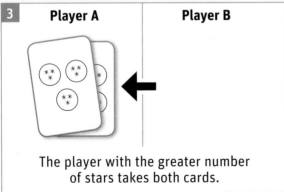

3

| Player A | Player B |

The player with the greater number
of stars takes both cards.

➤ **When all the cards have been played, the winner
is the player who has the most cards.**

Circles and Stars Capture

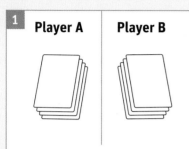

1 | Player A | Player B

Start with 9 cards each. Place them facedown in a pile.

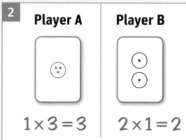

2 | Player A | Player B

$1 \times 3 = 3$ | $2 \times 1 = 2$

Turn over one card each. Write both multiplication equations.

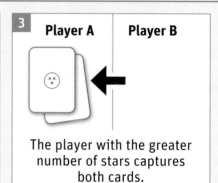

3 | Player A | Player B

The player with the greater number of stars captures both cards.

Player A	Player B

Circles and Stars Capture

HOW TO PLAY

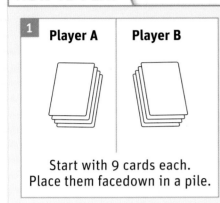

1

Player A	Player B

Start with 9 cards each.
Place them facedown in a pile.

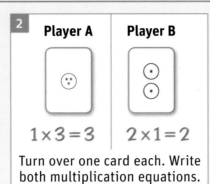

2

Player A	Player B

$1 \times 3 = 3$ $2 \times 1 = 2$

Turn over one card each. Write
both multiplication equations.

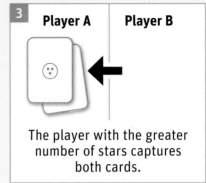

3

Player A	Player B

The player with the greater
number of stars captures
both cards.

Player A	Player B

Number Cube Products

DIRECTIONS

➤ Complete.

1 × 1 = _____   4 × 1 = _____

1 × 2 = _____   4 × 2 = _____

1 × 3 = _____   4 × 3 = _____

1 × 4 = _____   4 × 4 = _____

1 × 5 = _____   4 × 5 = _____

1 × 6 = _____   4 × 6 = _____

2 × 1 = _____   5 × 1 = _____

2 × 2 = _____   5 × 2 = _____

2 × 3 = _____   5 × 3 = _____

2 × 4 = _____   5 × 4 = _____

2 × 5 = _____   5 × 5 = _____

2 × 6 = _____   5 × 6 = _____

3 × 1 = _____   6 × 1 = _____

3 × 2 = _____   6 × 2 = _____

3 × 3 = _____   6 × 3 = _____

3 × 4 = _____   6 × 4 = _____

3 × 5 = _____   6 × 5 = _____

3 × 6 = _____   6 × 6 = _____

Number Cube Products

➤ Complete.

1. What is the greatest product for the factors 1 to 6? _____

2. What is the least product for the factors 1 to 6? _____

3. Which numbers from 1 to 36 are possible products from rolling two number cubes? Circle them.

1	2	3	4	5	6
7	8	9	10	11	12
13	14	15	16	17	18
19	20	21	22	23	24
25	26	27	28	29	30
31	32	33	34	35	36

4. List the products that appear only one time in the equations on page 16:

_____

5. List the products that appear exactly two times in the equations on page 16:

_____

6. List the products that appear more than two times in the equations on page 16:

_____

Game Rules for Multiplication Bingo

HOW TO PLAY

What you need

- number cubes (red, 1–6)
- *WorkSpace* pages 16, 17, 19, and 20

➤ Use the products from *WorkSpace* pages 16 and 17 to fill in all the squares on your *Bingo* card.

➤ Players take turns. Each turn has three steps.

1

The teacher rolls two number cubes and calls out the numbers.

2

$$2 \times 5 = 10$$

Write the multiplication equation.

3

B	I	N	G	O
4	15	4	6	25
36	12	9	16	2
7	24	FREE	8	18
10	9	30	10	15
20	3	16	36	4

If the product is on your *Bingo* card, mark it. Mark only one square per turn.

➤ The winner is the first player to get five Xs in a row.

Multiplication Bingo

UNIT 1

DIRECTIONS

1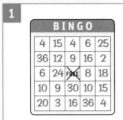
Write products in every square.

2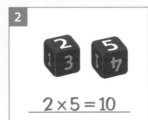
$$2 \times 5 = 10$$
Write the multiplication equation.

3
Mark out the product.

4
Bingo!
5 in a row wins.

BINGO

		FREE		

MULTIPLICATION EQUATIONS

Multiplication Bingo

DIRECTIONS

1

Write products in every square.

2

$2 \times 5 = 10$

Write the multiplication equation.

3

Mark out the product.

4

Bingo!

5 in a row wins.

BINGO

		FREE		

MULTIPLICATION EQUATIONS

Groups of Zero

DIRECTIONS

➤ Write the products.

➤ Write an addition equation for each multiplication equation.

① $1 \times 0 =$ ☐

② $2 \times 0 =$ ☐ _____

③ $3 \times 0 =$ ☐ _____

④ $4 \times 0 =$ ☐ _____

⑤ $5 \times 0 =$ ☐ _____

⑥ $6 \times 0 =$ ☐ _____

➤ Answer the questions.

⑦ Any number times zero equals _____.

Why? _____

⑧ What products from page 16 should not be on a *Multiplication Bingo* card when

the cubes will be 0–5 and 1–6? _____

Why? _____

⑨ What products can you write on a *Multiplication Bingo* card when the cubes

will be 0–5 and 1–6? _____

Multiplication Bingo With Zeros

DIRECTIONS

1

Write products in every square.

2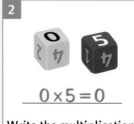

$0 \times 5 = 0$

Write the multiplication equation.

3

Mark out the product.

4

Bingo!

5 in a row wins.

BINGO

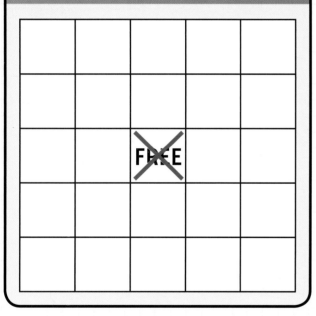

FREE

MULTIPLICATION EQUATIONS

Multiplication Bingo With Zeros

UNIT 1

DIRECTIONS

1
Write products in every square.

2
$$0 \times 5 = 0$$
Write the multiplication equation.

3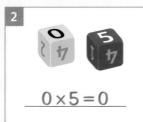
Mark out the product.

4
Bingo!
5 in a row wins.

BINGO

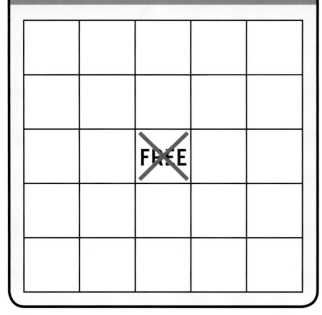

FREE

MULTIPLICATION EQUATIONS

Multiplying by 10

➤ Write the missing products.

① $1 \times 10 = \boxed{}$

② $5 \times 10 = \boxed{}$

③ $10 \times 12 = \boxed{}$

④ $7 \times 10 = \boxed{}$

⑤ $10 \times 3 = \boxed{}$

⑥ $11 \times 10 = \boxed{}$

⑦ $10 \times 8 = \boxed{}$

⑧ $2 \times 10 = \boxed{}$

⑨ $4 \times 10 = \boxed{}$

⑩ $9 \times 10 = \boxed{}$

⑪ $6 \times 10 = \boxed{}$

⑫ $12 \times 10 = \boxed{}$

⑬ $10 \times 11 = \boxed{}$

⑭ $10 \times 5 = \boxed{}$

➤ In the box below, show how you can figure out the product of 6×10.

⑮ $6 \times 10 = \boxed{}$

Show What You Know

➤ Write the product.

① $0 \times 4 =$ ☐

② $3 \times 5 =$ ☐

③ $6 \times 3 =$ ☐

④ $3 \times 1 =$ ☐

⑤ $6 \times 0 =$ ☐

⑥ $3 \times 6 =$ ☐

⑦ $4 \times 4 =$ ☐

⑧ $5 \times 2 =$ ☐

⑨ $6 \times 5 =$ ☐

⑩ $3 \times 4 =$ ☐

⑪ $4 \times 6 =$ ☐

⑫ $3 \times 3 =$ ☐

➤ Write one of the equations from above in the EQUATION box.

➤ Underline the product.

➤ Circle the factors.

➤ Show two different ways to figure.

⑬ **EQUATION**

⑭ **FIGURING**

Circles and Stars Capture

1

Player A	Player B

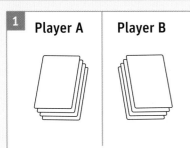

Start with 9 cards each.
Place them facedown in a pile.

2

Player A	Player B

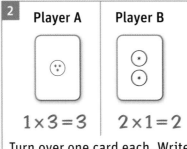

$1 \times 3 = 3$ | $2 \times 1 = 2$

Turn over one card each. Write
both multiplication equations.

3

Player A	Player B

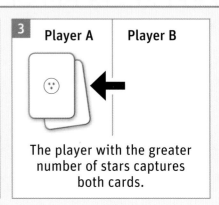

The player with the greater
number of stars captures
both cards.

Player A	Player B

Circles and Stars Capture

HOW TO PLAY

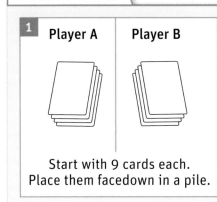

1 | Player A | Player B

Start with 9 cards each. Place them facedown in a pile.

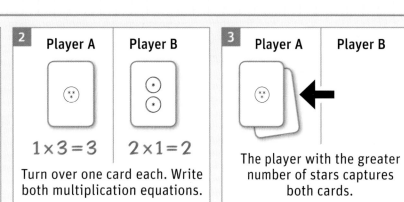

2 | Player A | Player B

$1 \times 3 = 3$ $2 \times 1 = 2$

Turn over one card each. Write both multiplication equations.

3 | Player A | Player B

The player with the greater number of stars captures both cards.

Player A	Player B

Which Has More Tiles?

DIRECTIONS

1

_3_ rows with

_2_ tiles in each row.

Complete the descriptions.

2

$2 + 2 + 2 = 6$

$2, 4, 6$

Three groups of two equals six

Use numbers, words, and pictures to show at least two different ways to figure the products.

3

_3_ rows with

_2_ tiles in each row.

$3 \times 2 = 6$

Write the equation.

4

$\boxed{3 \times 2 = 6}$

$3 \times 1 = 3$

Circle the equation for more tiles.

_____ rows with

_____ tiles in each row

_____ rows with

_____ tiles in each row

FIGURING

Which Has More Tiles?

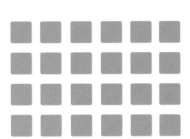

_____ rows with

_____ tiles in each row

_____ rows with

_____ tiles in each row

_____ rows with

_____ tiles in each row

_____ rows with

_____ tiles in each row

FIGURING

Equal Rows

DIRECTIONS

1

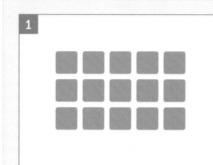

Look at the tiles.

2

$$3 \times 5 = 15$$

Write a multiplication equation for the group of tiles.

3

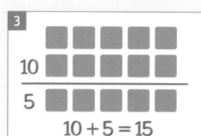

$$10 + 5 = 15$$

Explain with words, pictures, or numbers how you figured the number of tiles without counting them.

	Equation	Figuring

	Equation	Figuring

Game Rules for Tiles Capture

HOW TO PLAY

What you need

- *Tiles Capture* cards, 9 for each player
- *WorkSpace* pages 32 and 33 or blank paper

➤ **Each turn has three steps.**

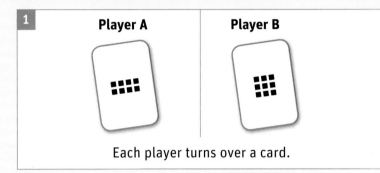

1

Player A	Player B

Each player turns over a card.

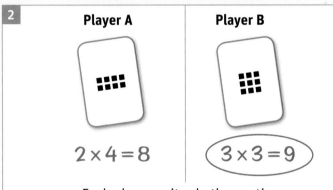

2

Player A	Player B

$$2 \times 4 = 8 \qquad \boxed{3 \times 3 = 9}$$

Each player writes both equations,
and circles the equation with the greater product.

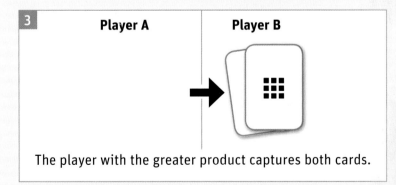

3

Player A	Player B

The player with the greater product captures both cards.

➤ **When all the cards have been played, the winner is the player with the most cards.**

Tiles Capture

HOW TO PLAY

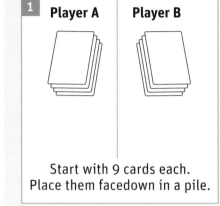

1

| Player A | Player B |

Start with 9 cards each.
Place them facedown in a pile.

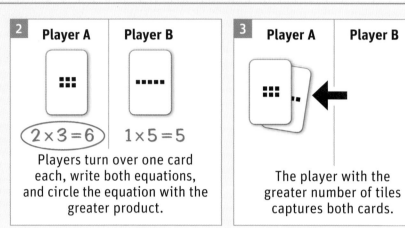

2

| Player A | Player B |

$2 \times 3 = 6$ $1 \times 5 = 5$

Players turn over one card
each, write both equations,
and circle the equation with the
greater product.

3

| Player A | Player B |

The player with the
greater number of tiles
captures both cards.

Player A	Player B

Tiles Capture

HOW TO PLAY

1 **Player A** **Player B**

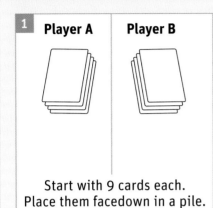

Start with 9 cards each.
Place them facedown in a pile.

2 **Player A** **Player B**

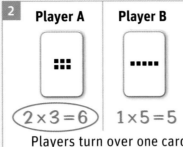

$2 \times 3 = 6$ $1 \times 5 = 5$

Players turn over one card each, write both equations, and circle the equation with the greater product.

3 **Player A** **Player B**

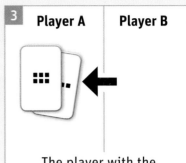

The player with the greater number of tiles captures both cards.

Player A	Player B

Find Products on the Multiplication Chart

DIRECTIONS

➤ Use the multiplication chart to find each product.

✕	1	2	3	4	5	6	7	8	9	10	11	12
1	1	2	3	4	5	6	7	8	9	10	11	12
2	2	4	6	8	10	12	14	16	18	20	22	24
3	3	6	9	12	15	18	21	24	27	30	33	36
4	4	8	12	16	20	24	28	32	36	40	44	48
5	5	10	15	20	25	30	35	40	45	50	55	60
6	6	12	18	24	30	36	42	48	54	60	66	72
7	7	14	21	28	35	42	49	56	63	70	77	84
8	8	16	24	32	40	48	56	64	72	80	88	96
9	9	18	27	36	45	54	63	72	81	90	99	108
10	10	20	30	40	50	60	70	80	90	100	110	120
11	11	22	33	44	55	66	77	88	99	110	121	132
12	12	24	36	48	60	72	84	96	108	120	132	144

1. $5 \times 7 = $ ☐

2. $6 \times 10 = $ ☐

3. $8 \times 8 = $ ☐

4. $4 \times 7 = $ ☐

5. $3 \times 9 = $ ☐

6. $2 \times 12 = $ ☐

7. $9 \times 9 = $ ☐

8. $6 \times 7 = $ ☐

9. $1 \times 11 = $ ☐

10. $12 \times 9 = $ ☐

11. $10 \times 10 = $ ☐

12. $5 \times 12 = $ ☐

Show What You Know

DIRECTIONS

1

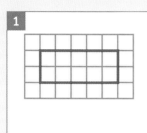

Draw each rectangle you build with 10 tiles.

2

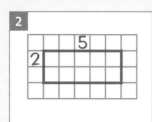

Label the rectangle.

3

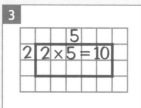

Write an equation in the rectangle.

Here is an example with 8 tiles.

	4	
2	$2 \times 4 = 8$	

Show What You Know

DIRECTIONS

➤ Use the multiplication chart to find the products.

X	1	2	3	4	5	6	7	8	9	10	11	12
1	1	2	3	4	5	6	7	8	9	10	11	12
2	2	4	6	8	10	12	14	16	18	20	22	24
3	3	6	9	12	15	18	21	24	27	30	33	36
4	4	8	12	16	20	24	28	32	36	40	44	48
5	5	10	15	20	25	30	35	40	45	50	55	60
6	6	12	18	24	30	36	42	48	54	60	66	72
7	7	14	21	28	35	42	49	56	63	70	77	84
8	8	16	24	32	40	48	56	64	72	80	88	96
9	9	18	27	36	45	54	63	72	81	90	99	108
10	10	20	30	40	50	60	70	80	90	100	110	120
11	11	22	33	44	55	66	77	88	99	110	121	132
12	12	24	36	48	60	72	84	96	108	120	132	144

1. $8 \times 6 =$
2. $2 \times 9 =$
3. $3 \times 8 =$
4. $9 \times 9 =$
5. $11 \times 4 =$
6. $5 \times 10 =$
7. $8 \times 8 =$
8. $12 \times 10 =$
9. $6 \times 6 =$
10. $5 \times 3 =$
11. $7 \times 4 =$
12. $10 \times 3 =$
13. $9 \times 8 =$
14. $6 \times 5 =$
15. $2 \times 12 =$

Tiles Capture

HOW TO PLAY

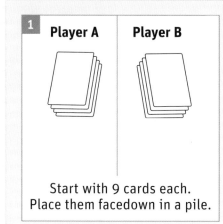

1

Player A	Player B

Start with 9 cards each.
Place them facedown in a pile.

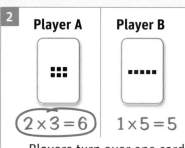

2

Player A	Player B

$2 \times 3 = 6$ | $1 \times 5 = 5$

Players turn over one card
each, write both multiplication
equations, and circle the equation
with the greater product.

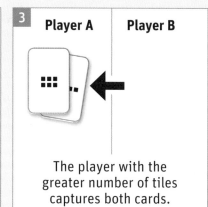

3

Player A	Player B

The player with the
greater number of tiles
captures both cards.

Player A	Player B

Growing Pattern of 6s

> Your teacher will tell you what to draw on the grid.

Equations With a Second Factor of 6

➤ Write the missing products and equations.

1 × 6 = ☐

2 × 6 = ☐

3 × 6 = ☐

4 × 6 = ☐

5 × 6 = ☐

___ × ___ = ☐

___ × ___ = ☐

___ × ___ = ☐

___ × ___ = ☐

___ × ___ = ☐

___ × ___ = ☐

___ × ___ = ☐

13 × 6 = 78

14 × 6 = 84

15 × 6 = ☐

16 × 6 = 96

17 × 6 = 102

18 × 6 = ☐

19 × 6 = 114

___ × ___ = ☐

21 × 6 = 126

___ × ___ = ☐

23 × 6 = 138

___ × ___ = ☐

Multiples of 6

DIRECTIONS

➤ Color all the multiples of 6 on this chart. Use your products from page 39.

✕	1	2	3	4	5	6	7	8	9	10	11	12
1	1	2	3	4	5	6	7	8	9	10	11	12
2	2	4	6	8	10	12	14	16	18	20	22	24
3	3	6	9	12	15	18	21	24	27	30	33	36
4	4	8	12	16	20	24	28	32	36	40	44	48
5	5	10	15	20	25	30	35	40	45	50	55	60
6	6	12	18	24	30	36	42	48	54	60	66	72
7	7	14	21	28	35	42	49	56	63	70	77	84
8	8	16	24	32	40	48	56	64	72	80	88	96
9	9	18	27	36	45	54	63	72	81	90	99	108
10	10	20	30	40	50	60	70	80	90	100	110	120
11	11	22	33	44	55	66	77	88	99	110	121	132
12	12	24	36	48	60	72	84	96	108	120	132	144

Multiples of 5

➤ Write the missing products.

$1 \times 5 = \boxed{}$

$2 \times 5 = \boxed{}$

$3 \times 5 = \boxed{}$

$4 \times 5 = \boxed{}$

$5 \times 5 = \boxed{}$

$6 \times 5 = \boxed{}$

$7 \times 5 = \boxed{}$

$8 \times 5 = \boxed{}$

$9 \times 5 = \boxed{}$

$10 \times 5 = \boxed{}$

$11 \times 5 = \boxed{}$

$12 \times 5 = \boxed{}$

$13 \times 5 = 65$

$14 \times 5 = \boxed{}$

$15 \times 5 = 75$

$16 \times 5 = \boxed{}$

$17 \times 5 = 85$

$18 \times 5 = 90$

$19 \times 5 = 95$

$20 \times 5 = \boxed{}$

$21 \times 5 = 105$

$22 \times 5 = 110$

$23 \times 5 = 115$

$24 \times 5 = \boxed{}$

$25 \times 5 = 125$

$26 \times 5 = 130$

$27 \times 5 = 135$

$28 \times 5 = 140$

Multiples of 5

DIRECTIONS

➤ Color the multiples of 5 on this chart. Use your products from page 41.

X	1	2	3	4	5	6	7	8	9	10	11	12
1	1	2	3	4	5	6	7	8	9	10	11	12
2	2	4	6	8	10	12	14	16	18	20	22	24
3	3	6	9	12	15	18	21	24	27	30	33	36
4	4	8	12	16	20	24	28	32	36	40	44	48
5	5	10	15	20	25	30	35	40	45	50	55	60
6	6	12	18	24	30	36	42	48	54	60	66	72
7	7	14	21	28	35	42	49	56	63	70	77	84
8	8	16	24	32	40	48	56	64	72	80	88	96
9	9	18	27	36	45	54	63	72	81	90	99	108
10	10	20	30	40	50	60	70	80	90	100	110	120
11	11	22	33	44	55	66	77	88	99	110	121	132
12	12	24	36	48	60	72	84	96	108	120	132	144

Multiples of 4

➤ **Write the missing products.**

$1 \times 4 = \boxed{}$

$2 \times 4 = \boxed{}$

$3 \times 4 = \boxed{}$

$4 \times 4 = \boxed{}$

$5 \times 4 = \boxed{}$

$6 \times 4 = \boxed{}$

$7 \times 4 = \boxed{}$

$8 \times 4 = \boxed{}$

$9 \times 4 = \boxed{}$

$10 \times 4 = \boxed{}$

$11 \times 4 = \boxed{}$

$12 \times 4 = \boxed{}$

$13 \times 4 = 52$

$14 \times 4 = 56$

$15 \times 4 = \boxed{}$

$16 \times 4 = 64$

$17 \times 4 = 68$

$18 \times 4 = \boxed{}$

$19 \times 4 = 76$

$20 \times 4 = \boxed{}$

$21 \times 4 = 84$

$22 \times 4 = 88$

$23 \times 4 = 92$

$24 \times 4 = 96$

$25 \times 4 = \boxed{}$

$26 \times 4 = 104$

$27 \times 4 = 108$

$28 \times 4 = 112$

$29 \times 4 = 116$

$30 \times 4 = \boxed{}$

$31 \times 4 = 124$

$32 \times 4 = 128$

$33 \times 4 = 132$

$34 \times 4 = 136$

$35 \times 4 = \boxed{}$

$36 \times 4 = 144$

UNIT 2

Multiples of 4

> Color the multiples of 4 on this chart. Use your products from page 43.

X	1	2	3	4	5	6	7	8	9	10	11	12
1	1	2	3	4	5	6	7	8	9	10	11	12
2	2	4	6	8	10	12	14	16	18	20	22	24
3	3	6	9	12	15	18	21	24	27	30	33	36
4	4	8	12	16	20	24	28	32	36	40	44	48
5	5	10	15	20	25	30	35	40	45	50	55	60
6	6	12	18	24	30	36	42	48	54	60	66	72
7	7	14	21	28	35	42	49	56	63	70	77	84
8	8	16	24	32	40	48	56	64	72	80	88	96
9	9	18	27	36	45	54	63	72	81	90	99	108
10	10	20	30	40	50	60	70	80	90	100	110	120
11	11	22	33	44	55	66	77	88	99	110	121	132
12	12	24	36	48	60	72	84	96	108	120	132	144

Multiples of 10

DIRECTIONS

➤ Write the missing products.

$1 \times 10 = \boxed{}$

$2 \times 10 = \boxed{}$

$3 \times 10 = \boxed{}$

$4 \times 10 = \boxed{}$

$5 \times 10 = \boxed{}$

$6 \times 10 = \boxed{}$

$7 \times 10 = \boxed{}$

$8 \times 10 = \boxed{}$

$9 \times 10 = \boxed{}$

$10 \times 10 = \boxed{}$

$11 \times 10 = \boxed{}$

$12 \times 10 = \boxed{}$

$13 \times 10 = 130$

$14 \times 10 = 140$

Explain how you find the product when you multiply by 10.

_____

_____

_____

Multiples of 10

DIRECTIONS

➤ Color the multiples of 10 on this chart. Use your products from page 45.

✕	1	2	3	4	5	6	7	8	9	10	11	12
1	1	2	3	4	5	6	7	8	9	10	11	12
2	2	4	6	8	10	12	14	16	18	20	22	24
3	3	6	9	12	15	18	21	24	27	30	33	36
4	4	8	12	16	20	24	28	32	36	40	44	48
5	5	10	15	20	25	30	35	40	45	50	55	60
6	6	12	18	24	30	36	42	48	54	60	66	72
7	7	14	21	28	35	42	49	56	63	70	77	84
8	8	16	24	32	40	48	56	64	72	80	88	96
9	9	18	27	36	45	54	63	72	81	90	99	108
10	10	20	30	40	50	60	70	80	90	100	110	120
11	11	22	33	44	55	66	77	88	99	110	121	132
12	12	24	36	48	60	72	84	96	108	120	132	144

Cross Out Products

DIRECTIONS

➤ Draw a line through the products that are easy for you to figure out or remember.

➤ Draw a line through the products you know.

➤ Draw a line through products that are the same because of the Commutative Property.

➤ Circle the remaining products.

✕	1	2	3	4	5	6	7	8	9	10	11	12
1	1	2	3	4	5	6	7	8	9	10	11	12
2	2	4	6	8	10	12	14	16	18	20	22	24
3	3	6	9	12	15	18	21	24	27	30	33	36
4	4	8	12	16	20	24	28	32	36	40	44	48
5	5	10	15	20	25	30	35	40	45	50	55	60
6	6	12	18	24	30	36	42	48	54	60	66	72
7	7	14	21	28	35	42	49	56	63	70	77	84
8	8	16	24	32	40	48	56	64	72	80	88	96
9	9	18	27	36	45	54	63	72	81	90	99	108
10	10	20	30	40	50	60	70	80	90	100	110	120
11	11	22	33	44	55	66	77	88	99	110	121	132
12	12	24	36	48	60	72	84	96	108	120	132	144

Multiplication Facts to Learn

> DIRECTIONS

➤ Choose ten of the circled products from your chart on page 47.

➤ Write equations for the ten products.

➤ Practice them during the week.

➤ When you learn a fact, cross it off and write a new one.

① _____

② _____

③ _____

④ _____

⑤ _____

⑥ _____

⑦ _____

⑧ _____

⑨ _____

⑩ _____

Show What You Know

➤ Complete.

Write equations that have a first factor of 3. Start with 3 × 1 and go to 3 × 12.

① ___3 × 1 = 3___   ⑤ _____   ⑨ _____

② _____   ⑥ _____   ⑩ _____

③ _____   ⑦ _____   ⑪ _____

④ _____   ⑧ _____   ⑫ _____

Write the multiples of 6 to 72.

⑬ __6__ ___ ___ ___ ___ ___ ___ ___ ___ ___ ___ _72_

Write the multiples of 4 to 48.

⑭ __4__ ___ ___ ___ ___ ___ ___ ___ ___ ___ ___ _48_

⑮ If 4 × 21 = 84, what is 4 × 22? _____

⑯ If 6 × 15 = 90, what is 6 × 16? _____

⑰ If 5 × 22 = 110, what is 5 × 23? _____

⑱ If 6 × 17 = 102, what is 6 × 18? _____

⑲ If 8 × 18 = 144, what is 8 × 19? _____

⑳ Explain how you used 8 × 18 = 144 to solve 8 × 19.

_____

_____

Equations With Your Assigned Factor

DIRECTIONS

➤ Choose 7, 8, 9, or 12. Fill in that number as the second factor in each equation. Then write the product for each.

1   × _____ = ☐

2   × _____ = ☐

3   × _____ = ☐

4   × _____ = ☐

5   × _____ = ☐

6   × _____ = ☐

7   × _____ = ☐

8   × _____ = ☐

9   × _____ = ☐

10 × _____ = ☐

11 × _____ = ☐

12 × _____ = ☐

13 × _____ = ☐

14 × _____ = ☐

15 × _____ = ☐

16 × _____ = ☐

17 × _____ = ☐

18 × _____ = ☐

19 × _____ = ☐

20 × _____ = ☐

21 × _____ = ☐

22 × _____ = ☐

23 × _____ = ☐

24 × _____ = ☐

25 × _____ = ☐

26 × _____ = ☐

27 × _____ = ☐

28 × _____ = ☐

Multiples of ___

➤ Use your products from page 50 with first factors from 1–12.
Shade in those products on this chart.

X	1	2	3	4	5	6	7	8	9	10	11	12
1	1	2	3	4	5	6	7	8	9	10	11	12
2	2	4	6	8	10	12	14	16	18	20	22	24
3	3	6	9	12	15	18	21	24	27	30	33	36
4	4	8	12	16	20	24	28	32	36	40	44	48
5	5	10	15	20	25	30	35	40	45	50	55	60
6	6	12	18	24	30	36	42	48	54	60	66	72
7	7	14	21	28	35	42	49	56	63	70	77	84
8	8	16	24	32	40	48	56	64	72	80	88	96
9	9	18	27	36	45	54	63	72	81	90	99	108
10	10	20	30	40	50	60	70	80	90	100	110	120
11	11	22	33	44	55	66	77	88	99	110	121	132
12	12	24	36	48	60	72	84	96	108	120	132	144

UNIT 2

Equations With Your Own Factor

DIRECTIONS

➤ Choose a different factor (7, 8, 9, or 12) from the one you used on page 50. Fill in that number as the second factor in each equation. Then write the product for each.

1   × _____ = ☐   15   × _____ = ☐

2   × _____ = ☐   16   × _____ = ☐

3   × _____ = ☐   17   × _____ = ☐

4   × _____ = ☐   18   × _____ = ☐

5   × _____ = ☐   19   × _____ = ☐

6   × _____ = ☐   20   × _____ = ☐

7   × _____ = ☐   21   × _____ = ☐

8   × _____ = ☐   22   × _____ = ☐

9   × _____ = ☐   23   × _____ = ☐

10   × _____ = ☐   24   × _____ = ☐

11   × _____ = ☐   25   × _____ = ☐

12   × _____ = ☐   26   × _____ = ☐

13   × _____ = ☐   27   × _____ = ☐

14   × _____ = ☐   28   × _____ = ☐

Multiples of ____

DIRECTIONS

➤ Use your products from page 52 with first factors from 1–12.
   Shade in those products on this chart.

✕	1	2	3	4	5	6	7	8	9	10	11	12
1	1	2	3	4	5	6	7	8	9	10	11	12
2	2	4	6	8	10	12	14	16	18	20	22	24
3	3	6	9	12	15	18	21	24	27	30	33	36
4	4	8	12	16	20	24	28	32	36	40	44	48
5	5	10	15	20	25	30	35	40	45	50	55	60
6	6	12	18	24	30	36	42	48	54	60	66	72
7	7	14	21	28	35	42	49	56	63	70	77	84
8	8	16	24	32	40	48	56	64	72	80	88	96
9	9	18	27	36	45	54	63	72	81	90	99	108
10	10	20	30	40	50	60	70	80	90	100	110	120
11	11	22	33	44	55	66	77	88	99	110	121	132
12	12	24	36	48	60	72	84	96	108	120	132	144

Grid Paper

Draw Rectangles and Figure Products

3×4

1

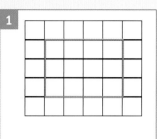

Draw a rectangle on the grid.

2

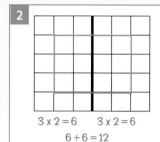

$3 \times 2 = 6$ $3 \times 2 = 6$

$6 + 6 = 12$

Figure the product without counting

3

$3 \times 4 = 12$

Write the equation.

8×4 10×6 9×5

6×7 5×8 5×7

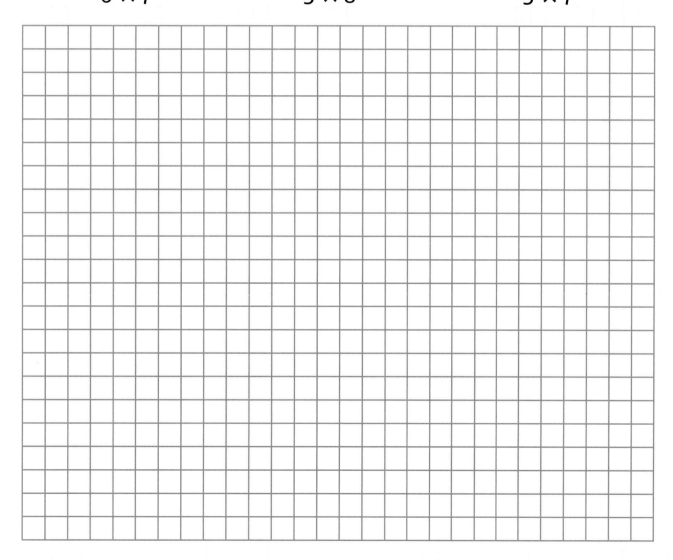

Rectangle Splitting: 11

DIRECTIONS

➤ Draw a rectangle to match the multiplication problem.

➤ Split the rectangle to make two easier problems.

➤ Write equations for your split rectangle.

➤ Write the product in the box for each equation.

11 × 8 = ☐   11 × 9 = ☐   11 × 13 = ☐

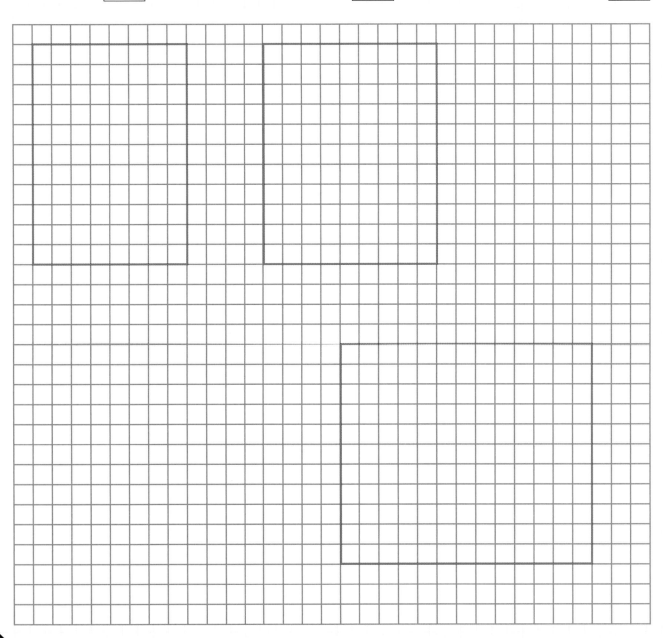

Number Splitting: 11

11×12

1
$$11 = 10 + 1$$
$$10 \times 12 = 120$$
$$1 \times 12 = 12$$

Split a factor and write two equations.

2
$$120 + 12 = 132$$

Add the products of the two equations.

3
$$11 \times 12 = \boxed{132}$$

Write the product.

UNIT 2

---

① 11×14

Equation 1 _____

Equation 2 _____

Add the products.

_____

Write the product. $11 \times 14 = \boxed{}$

---

② 11×17

Equation 1 _____

Equation 2 _____

Add the products.

_____

Write the product. $11 \times 17 = \boxed{}$

Split the rectangles below to show how you split the numbers in 1 and 2.

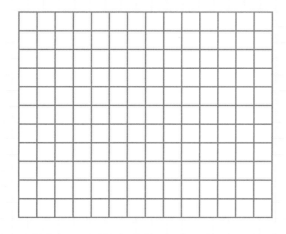

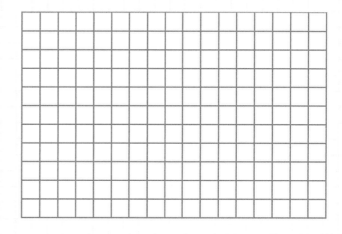

Rectangle Splitting: 12

DIRECTIONS

➤ Draw a rectangle to match the multiplication problem.
➤ Split the rectangle to make two easier problems.
➤ Write equations for your split rectangle.
➤ Write the product in the box for each equation.

12 × 6 = ☐   12 × 8 = ☐   12 × 13 = ☐

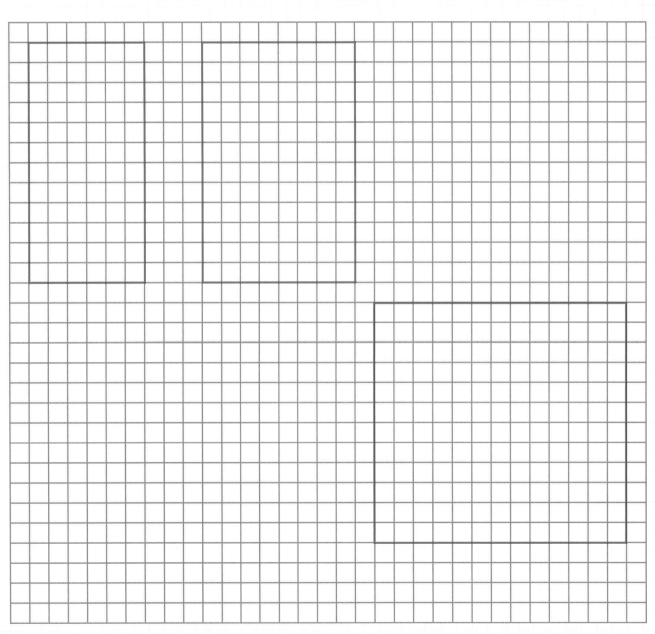

Number Splitting: 12

➤ Write two equations for each problem.

➤ Add the products.

➤ Write the product of the original problem.

➤ Do problem 1 as your teacher writes the equations on the board.

UNIT 2

---

(1) 12 × 15

Equation 1 _____

Equation 2 _____

Add the products.

_____

Write the product.   12 × 15 = ☐

---

(3) 12 × 16

Equation 1 _____

Equation 2 _____

Add the products.

_____

Write the product.   12 × 16 = ☐

---

(2) 12 × 14

Equation 1 _____

Equation 2 _____

Add the products.

_____

Write the product.   12 × 14 = ☐

---

(4) 12 × 13

Equation 1 _____

Equation 2 _____

Add the products.

_____

Write the product.   12 × 13 = ☐

Number Splitting With a Factor of 12

1

$12 \times 2 = \boxed{24}$

Write the product from memory if you can.

2

$10 \times 2 = 20$
$2 \times 2 = 4$
$20 + 4 = 24$

Show that the product is correct using number splitting.

3

$12 \times 15 = \boxed{180}$
$10 \times 15 = 150$
$2 \times 15 = 30$
$150 + 30 = 180$
$12 \times 15 = 180$

If you don't know the product, use number splitting to figure the product.

① $12 \times 3 = \boxed{}$

④ $12 \times 6 = \boxed{}$

⑦ $12 \times 9 = \boxed{}$

② $12 \times 4 = \boxed{}$

⑤ $12 \times 7 = \boxed{}$

⑧ $12 \times 11 = \boxed{}$

③ $12 \times 5 = \boxed{}$

⑥ $12 \times 8 = \boxed{}$

⑨ $12 \times 12 = \boxed{}$

Show What You Know

DIRECTIONS

➤ Write the products.

① 12 × 12 = ☐

⑤ 12 × 10 = ☐

② 11 × 7 = ☐

⑥ 12 × 5 = ☐

③ 11 × 10 = ☐

⑦ 12 × 11 = ☐

④ 11 × 12 = ☐

⑧ 11 × 13 = ☐

➤ Use the number-splitting strategy to find the product. Write each equation.

⑨ 12 × 13

_____

_____

_____

_____

Show What You Know

DIRECTIONS

➤ Write the products.

① 3 × 3 = ☐

② 3 × 6 = ☐

③ 4 × 4 = ☐

④ 8 × 7 = ☐

⑤ 6 × 0 = ☐

⑥ 6 × 8 = ☐

⑦ 12 × 2 = ☐

⑧ 2 × 12 = ☐

⑨ 12 × 8 = ☐

⑩ 6 × 6 = ☐

⑪ 6 × 12 = ☐

⑫ 12 × 6 = ☐

⑬ 7 × 6 = ☐

⑭ 7 × 12 = ☐

⑮ 8 × 4 = ☐

⑯ 8 × 8 = ☐

⑰ 8 × 5 = ☐

⑱ 8 × 10 = ☐

⑲ 9 × 4 = ☐

⑳ 9 × 8 = ☐

㉑ 9 × 3 = ☐

㉒ 9 × 6 = ☐

㉓ 12 × 3 = ☐

㉔ 7 × 3 = ☐

㉕ 12 × 12 = ☐

㉖ 9 × 9 = ☐

㉗ 10 × 10 = ☐

㉘ 11 × 4 = ☐

㉙ 11 × 8 = ☐

㉚ 7 × 7 = ☐

Game Rules for Pathways

What you need

- green tiles
- *WorkSpace* pages 64–67

1

Pathways Game Board

16	32	24	15	48
28	40	35	64	20
30	12	56	21	16
9	25	49	42	36

■ 4 5 ■ 7 8

Player X places two green tiles over factors, and draws an X on the product.

2

Pathways Game Board

16	32	24	15	48
28	40	35	64	20
30	12	56	21	16
9	25	49	42	36

■ 4 5 ■ 7 8

Player X	Player O
$3 \times 6 = 18$	

Player O checks that the product is correct.
Both players write the equation.

3

Pathways Game Board

16	32	(24)	15	48
28	40	35	64	20
30	12	56	21	16
9	25	49	42	36

3 ■ 5 ■ 7 8

Player X	Player O
$3 \times 6 = 18$	$4 \times 6 = 24$

Player O places a green tile over one new factor, and draws a O on the product. Player X checks the product, and both players write the equation.

➤ The winner is the first player to complete a path from top to bottom or from side to side of the game board.

UNIT 2

Pathways Game Board

18	32	24	15	48
28	40	35	64	20
30	12	56	21	16
9	25	49	42	36

3   4   5   6   7   8

A

18	32	24	15	48
28	40	35	64	20
30	12	56	21	16
9	25	49	42	36

3   4   5   6   7   8

A

18	32	24	15	48
28	40	35	64	20
30	12	56	21	16
9	25	49	42	36

3   4   5   6   7   8

A

18	32	24	15	48
28	40	35	64	20
30	12	56	21	16
9	25	49	42	36

3   4   5   6   7   8

Pathways Recording Sheet

DIRECTIONS

➤ Record your equations and your partner's equations.

Player X	Player O

Player X	Player O

Player X	Player O

Player X	Player O

Pathways Game Board

B

81	54	63	36	72
28	18	32	81	24
48	64	21	16	56
12	9	42	49	27

3　4　6　7　8　9

C

81	64	48	36	63
30	42	32	35	28
72	25	49	24	45
16	54	20	40	56

4　5　6　7　8　9

D

54	28	42	72	63
77	36	16	99	64
49	32	44	81	121
56	48	66	88	24

4　6　7　8　9　11

E

72	36	49	88	54
84	77	96	132	56
63	81	48	108	121
66	99	144	64	42

6　7　8　9　11　12

Pathways Recording Sheet

DIRECTIONS

➤ Record your equations and your partner's equations.

Player X	Player O

Player X	Player O

Player X	Player O

Player X	Player O

Three-Factor Problems

1

$$3 \times 2 \times 3$$

Look at the problem.

2

$3 \times 2 \times 3$
$6 \times 3 = 18$

$3 \times 2 \times 3$
$9 \times 2 = 18$

$3 \times 2 \times 3$
$3 \times 6 = 18$

Write and solve three two-factor problems.

$2 \times 2 \times 4$

More Three-Factor Problems

1

$3 \times 2 \times 3$

Look at the problem.

2

$3 \times 2 \times 3$
$6 \times 3 = 18$

$3 \times 2 \times 3$
$9 \times 2 = 18$

$3 \times 2 \times 3$
$3 \times 6 = 18$

Write and solve three two-factor problems.

① $2 \times 5 \times 4$

② $2 \times 6 \times 4$

③ $5 \times 2 \times 3$

④ $3 \times 5 \times 4$

UNIT 2

Solve Three-Factor Problems

DIRECTIONS

1

$3 \times 2 \times 3$

Look at the problem.

2

$3 \times 2 \times 3$
$6 \times 3 = 18$

$3 \times 2 \times 3$
$9 \times 2 = 18$

$3 \times 2 \times 3$
$3 \times 6 = 18$

Write and solve three two-factor problems.

① $2 \times 5 \times 3$

② $2 \times 5 \times 7$

③ $2 \times 5 \times 5$

④ $2 \times 8 \times 5$

Game Rules for Times 10

What you need

• green tiles
• *WorkSpace* pages 72–75

1

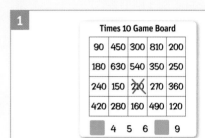

Player X places green tiles over two factors, and finds the product. Then Player X multiplies the product by 10 and draws an X on that square.

2

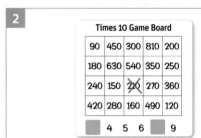

Player X	Player O
$3 \times 7 = 21$	
$21 \times 10 = 210$	

Player O checks that the product is correct. Both players write the equations.

3

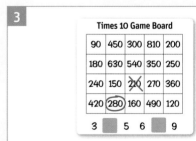

Player X	Player O
$3 \times 7 = 21$	$4 \times 7 = 28$
$21 \times 10 = 210$	$28 \times 10 = 280$

Player O places a green tile over one new factor, and multiplies the product of the factors by 10. Player O draws an O on the square. Player X checks the product. Both players write the equations.

➤ **The winner is the first player to complete a path from top to bottom or from side to side of the game board.**

UNIT 2

Times 10 Game Board

A

90	450	300	810	200
180	630	540	350	250
240	150	210	270	360
420	280	160	490	120

3 4 5 6 7 9

A

90	450	300	810	200
180	630	540	350	250
240	150	210	270	360
420	280	160	490	120

3 4 5 6 7 9

A

90	450	300	810	200
180	630	540	350	250
240	150	210	270	360
420	280	160	490	120

3 4 5 6 7 9

A

90	450	300	810	200
180	630	540	350	250
240	150	210	270	360
420	280	160	490	120

3 4 5 6 7 9

Times 10 Recording Sheet

➤ Record your equations and your partner's equations.

Player X	Player O

Player X	Player O

Player X	Player O

Player X	Player O

Times 10 Game Board

B

810	480	540	640	630
210	360	160	720	560
280	120	180	90	320
420	810	490	240	270

3   4   6   7   8   9

B

810	480	540	640	630
210	360	160	720	560
280	120	180	90	320
420	810	490	240	270

3   4   6   7   8   9

B

810	480	540	640	630
210	360	160	720	560
280	120	180	90	320
420	810	490	240	270

3   4   6   7   8   9

B

810	480	540	640	630
210	360	160	720	560
280	120	180	90	320
420	810	490	240	270

3   4   6   7   8   9

Times 10 Recording Sheet

➤ Record your equations and your partner's equations.

Player X	Player O

Player X	Player O

Player X	Player O

Player X	Player O

UNIT 2

Write a Two-Factor Problem as a Three-Factor Problem

1

7×40

$7 \times 4 \times 10$

Rewrite the multiple of 10 as the product of 10 and another factor.

2

7×40

$7 \times 4 \times 10$

$28 \times 10 = 280$

Multiply by 10 last.

3

7×40

$7 \times 4 \times 10$

$28 \times 10 = 280$

$7 \times 40 = 280$

Write the original problem with the product.

6×70

Explain how changing the two-factor problem into a three-factor problem helps you find the product.

_____

_____

Write Two-Factor Problems as Three-Factor Problems

1

7×40

$7 \times 4 \times 10$

Rewrite the multiple of 10 as the product of 10 and another factor.

2

7×40

$7 \times 4 \times 10$

$28 \times 10 = 280$

Multiply by 10 last.

3

7×40

$7 \times 4 \times 10$

$28 \times 10 = 280$

$7 \times 40 = 280$

Write the original problem with the product.

---

① 8×20

___ × ___ × ___

② 8×70

___ × ___ × ___

③ 3×50

___ × ___ × ___

④ 5×90

___ × ___ × ___

UNIT 2

⑤ 70 × 3

___ × ___ × ___

⑥ 80 × 9

⑦ 9 × 90

⑧ 80 × 4

⑨ 30 × 8

⑩ 60 × 7

Game Rules for Target 300

What you need

- number cube (red, 1–6)
- *WorkSpace* pages 80 and 81

➤ **The game is six turns.**

1

Player A rolls the number cube.

2

Player A	Score	Player B	Score
2 × 20 2 × 2 × 10 4 × 10 = 40	40		

Player A multiplies the number by 10, 20, 30, 40, or 50. Both players record the solution and score.

3

Player B rolls the number cube.

4

Player A	Score	Player B	Score
2 × 20 2 × 2 × 10 4 × 10 = 40	40	5 × 20 5 × 2 × 10 10 × 10 = 100	100

Player B multiplies the number by 10, 20, 30, 40, or 50. Both players record the solution and score.

➤ **Players add their amounts from each turn to their previous scores.**

➤ **The winner is the player whose score is closer to 300 after 6 turns.**

UNIT 2

Target 300

➤ Record your equations and scores and your partner's equations and scores.

Player A	Score	Player B	Score

_____ is _____ points from 300.

_____ is _____ points from 300.

_____ won the game.

UNIT 2

Target 300

➤ Record your equations and scores and your partner's equations and scores.

Player A	Score	Player B	Score

_____ is _____ points from 300.

_____ is _____ points from 300.

_____ won the game.

UNIT 2

Show What You Know

1

$$7 \times 40$$
$$7 \times 4 \times 10$$

Rewrite the multiple of 10 as the product of 10 and another factor.

2

$$7 \times 40$$
$$7 \times 4 \times 10$$
$$28 \times 10 = 280$$

Multiply by 10 last.

3

$$7 \times 40$$
$$7 \times 4 \times 10$$
$$28 \times 10 = 280$$
$$7 \times 40 = 280$$

Write the original problem with the product.

① 90×7

② 80×6

③ 8×70

④ 40×5

⑤ 4×90

⑥ 3×70

Show What You Know

① $10 \times 42 =$ _____

② $23 \times 10 =$ _____

③ $55 \times 10 =$ _____

④ $10 \times 39 =$ _____

⑤ $77 \times 10 =$ _____

⑥ $86 \times 10 =$ _____

⑦ $10 \times 34 =$ _____

⑧ $41 \times 10 =$ _____

⑨ $98 \times 10 =$ _____

⑩ $10 \times 62 =$ _____

Target 300

DIRECTIONS

➤ Record your equations and scores and your partner's equations and scores.

Player A	Score	Player B	Score

_____ is _____ points from 300.

_____ is _____ points from 300.

_____ won the game.

Use the Splitting Strategy

DIRECTIONS

1

$$16 \times 4$$

Look at the problem.

2

$10 \times 4 = 40$

$6 \times 4 = 24$

$40 + 24 = 64$

$16 \times 4 = 64$

Use splitting and write equations to solve the problem.

5×18

Use words or drawings to explain how you solved this problem.

Use the Splitting Strategy

1

$$16 \times 4$$

Look at the problem.

2

$$10 \times \ 4 = 40$$
$$6 \times \ 4 = 24$$
$$40 + 24 = 64$$
$$16 \times \ 4 = 64$$

Use splitting and write equations to solve the problem.

① 4×13

② 15×7

③ 2×19

④ 14×7

⑤ 16×6

⑥ 5×18

More Practice Using the Splitting Strategy

DIRECTIONS

1

8×14

Look at the problem.

2

$8 \times 10 = 80$
$8 \times 4 = 32$
$80 + 32 = 112$
$8 \times 14 = 112$

Use splitting and write
equations to solve the problem.

① 9×17

② 4×19

③ 16×7

④ 4×18

⑤ 6×17

⑥ 8×13

UNIT 3

Target 300

DIRECTIONS

➤ Record your equations and scores and your partner's equations and scores.

Player A	Score	Player B	Score

_____ is _____ points from 300.

_____ is _____ points from 300.

_____ won the game.

The Shortcut

➤ Write each product.

1. $20 \times 9 =$ _____

2. $4 \times 50 =$ _____

3. $9 \times 30 =$ _____

4. $7 \times 80 =$ _____

5. $60 \times 7 =$ _____

6. $80 \times 4 =$ _____

7. $50 \times 6 =$ _____

8. $4 \times 30 =$ _____

9. $60 \times 9 =$ _____

10. $40 \times 9 =$ _____

11. $3 \times 50 =$ _____

12. $90 \times 6 =$ _____

Target 300

DIRECTIONS

➤ Record your equations and scores and your partner's equations and scores.

Player A	Score	Player B	Score

_____ is _____ points from 300.

_____ is _____ points from 300.

_____ won the game.

Rules for Target 1000

What you need

- number cube (red, 1–6)
- *WorkSpace* pages 92 and 93

➤ **Players take turns.**

1

Player A rolls the number cube.

2

10   20   30   40   ~~50~~   60   70   80   90   100

$4 \times \underline{50} = 200$

Player A multiplies the number on the cube by one of the multiples of ten and then crosses out that number.

3

Player A hands the cube to Player B.

4

10   20   30   40   50   ~~60~~   70   80   90   100

$5 \times \underline{60} = 300$

Player B takes a turn.

➤ **Players add their answers from each turn to their previous scores.**

➤ **The winner is the player whose score is closer to 1000—without going over—after each player has taken six turns.**

UNIT 3

Target 1000

DIRECTIONS

➤ Record your equations and scores.

| 10 | 20 | 30 | 40 | 50 | 60 | 70 | 80 | 90 | 100 |

Number Rolled	Multiple of Ten	Equation	Score
Roll 1			
Roll 2			
Roll 3			
Roll 4			
Roll 5			
Roll 6			TOTAL

UNIT 3

Target 1000

➤ Record your equations and scores.

| 10 | 20 | 30 | 40 | 50 | 60 | 70 | 80 | 90 | 100 |

Number Rolled	Multiple of Ten	Equation	Score
Roll 1			
Roll 2			
Roll 3			
Roll 4			
Roll 5			
Roll 6			TOTAL

UNIT 3

Show What You Know

1

16×4

Look at the problem.

2

$10 \times 4 = 40$

$6 \times 4 = 24$

$40 + 24 = 64$

$16 \times 4 = 64$

Use splitting and write equations to solve the problem.

① 11×8

② 18×3

③ 5×15

④ 19×9

⑤ 4×17

⑥ 13×9

⑦ 14 × 5

⑧ 6 × 16

⑨ 17 × 8

⑩ 13 × 6

⑪ 7 × 18

⑫ 16 × 6

⑬ 15 × 8

⑭ 8 × 12

UNIT 3

Target 1000

DIRECTIONS

➤ Record your equations and scores.

| 10 | 20 | 30 | 40 | 50 | 60 | 70 | 80 | 90 | 100 |

Number Rolled	Multiple of Ten	Equation	Score
Roll 1			
Roll 2			
Roll 3			
Roll 4			
Roll 5			
Roll 6			TOTAL

Target 1000

DIRECTIONS

➤ Record your equations and scores.

| 10 | 20 | 30 | 40 | 50 | 60 | 70 | 80 | 90 | 100 |

Number Rolled	Multiple of Ten	Equation	Score
Roll 1			
Roll 2			
Roll 3			
Roll 4			
Roll 5			
Roll 6			
			TOTAL

UNIT 3

Multiply Multiples of 10

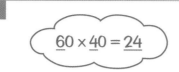

60×40

1

$\underline{6}0 \times \underline{4}0 = \underline{24}$

Think about a fact from the Multiplication Chart.

2

$60 \times 40 = 2400$

Think times 10, tack on zero; times 10, tack on another zero.

① $20 \times 40 =$ _____

② $60 \times 50 =$ _____

③ $90 \times 40 =$ _____

④ $30 \times 60 =$ _____

⑤ $80 \times 70 =$ _____

⑥ $90 \times 70 =$ _____

⑦ $50 \times 80 =$ _____

⑧ $20 \times 80 =$ _____

⑨ $20 \times 20 =$ _____

⑩ $60 \times 80 =$ _____

⑪ $40 \times 70 =$ _____

⑫ $30 \times 90 =$ _____

UNIT 3

Multiply Multiples of 10 and 100

DIRECTIONS

➤ Write each product.

① $6 \times 100 =$ _____

② $90 \times 60 =$ _____

③ $100 \times 9 =$ _____

④ $70 \times 70 =$ _____

⑤ $600 \times 6 =$ _____

⑥ $20 \times 50 =$ _____

⑦ $400 \times 8 =$ _____

⑧ $600 \times 9 =$ _____

⑨ $500 \times 4 =$ _____

⑩ $300 \times 7 =$ _____

⑪ $30 \times 40 =$ _____

⑫ $80 \times 80 =$ _____

⑬ $200 \times 4 =$ _____

⑭ $60 \times 70 =$ _____

⑮ $500 \times 7 =$ _____

⑯ $90 \times 40 =$ _____

⑰ $5 \times 300 =$ _____

⑱ $700 \times 8 =$ _____

⑲ $50 \times 80 =$ _____

⑳ $4 \times 800 =$ _____

UNIT 3

Use the Splitting Strategy

1

$$54 \times 7$$

Look at the problem.

2

$54 = 50 + 4$

$50 \times 7 = 350$

$4 \times 7 = 28$

$54 \times 7 = 378$

$$\begin{array}{r} 350 \\ +28 \\ \hline 378 \end{array}$$

Solve by splitting.

① 93×7

② 82×5

③ 17×6

④ 48×8

Make Estimates to Check Products

1

$$58 \times 7$$

$$60 \times 7 = 420$$

Make an estimate.

2

$$58 = 50 + 8$$
$$50 \times 7 = 350 \qquad 350$$
$$8 \times 7 = 56 \qquad +56$$
$$\overline{406}$$
$$58 \times 7 = 406$$

Use the splitting strategy
to solve the problem.

3

✓

Write a
check mark
if your answer
is close to
your estimate.

Make an estimate	Solve the problem	Check estimate
① 89 × 4		
② 21 × 3		
③ 49 × 6		

UNIT 3

Solve 37 × 6

1

$$58$$
$$\times\ 7$$

$$60 \times 7 = 420$$

Make an estimate.

2

$$58 = 50 + 8$$
$$58$$
$$\times 7$$
$$50 \times 7 = 350$$
$$8 \times 7 = \underline{56}$$
$$406$$

Solve the problem.

3

✓

Write a check mark if your answer is close to your estimate.

$$37$$
$$\times\ 6$$

My estimate

_____

Is your answer reasonable? _____

Explain how you made your estimate.

_____

_____

_____

_____

UNIT 3

Make Estimates to Check Products

1

58
× 7

60 × 7 = 420

Make an estimate.

2

58 = 50 + 8

58
× 7
50 × 7 = 350
8 × 7 = 56
406

Solve the problem.

3

✓

Write a
check mark
if your answer
is close to
your estimate.

Make an estimate	Solve the problem	Check estimate
① 75 × 9		
② 92 × 8		
③ 55 × 5		
④ 48 × 9		

UNIT 3

Show What You Know

➤ Write each product.

① $6 \times 40 =$ _____

② $5 \times 90 =$ _____

③ $18 \times 10 =$ _____

④ $50 \times 4 =$ _____

⑤ $70 \times 6 =$ _____

⑥ $2 \times 30 =$ _____

⑦ $3 \times 80 =$ _____

⑧ $7 \times 20 =$ _____

⑨ $30 \times 9 =$ _____

⑩ $7 \times 50 =$ _____

⑪ $8 \times 60 =$ _____

⑫ $90 \times 4 =$ _____

⑬ $70 \times 2 =$ _____

⑭ $5 \times 80 =$ _____

⑮ $9 \times 70 =$ _____

⑯ $60 \times 6 =$ _____

Show What You Know

1

$$58$$
$$\times\ 7$$

$$60 \times 7 = 420$$

Make an estimate.

2

$$58 = 50 + 8$$
$$58$$
$$\times 7$$
$$50 \times 7 = \overline{350}$$
$$8 \times 7 = \underline{\ 56}$$
$$406$$

Solve the problem.

3

✓

Write a check mark if your answer is close to your estimate.

Make an estimate	Solve the problem	Check estimate
① 78 × 3		
② 81 × 7		
③ 58 × 4		
④ 36 × 9		

UNIT 3

Target 1000

➤ Multiply the number you roll by 10, 20, 40, 60, or 80.

➤ Record your equations and scores and your partner's equations and scores.

Player A	Score	Player B	Score

_____ is _____ points from 1000.

_____ is _____ points from 1000.

_____ won the game.

Target 1000

➤ Multiply the number you roll by 10, 20, 40, 60, or 80.

➤ Record your equations and scores and your partner's equations and scores.

Player A	Score	Player B	Score

_____ is _____ points from 1000.

_____ is _____ points from 1000.

_____ won the game.

Multiply by Multiples of 100

① 2 × 300 = _____

② 900 × 4 = _____

③ 400 × 7 = _____

④ 500 × 9 = _____

⑤ 200 × 9 = _____

⑥ 300 × 8 = _____

⑦ 6 × 700 = _____

⑧ 6 × 800 = _____

⑨ 4 × 300 = _____

⑩ 300 × 7 = _____

⑪ 3 × 600 = _____

⑫ 700 × 8 = _____

⑬ 800 × 2 = _____

⑭ 5 × 400 = _____

⑮ 8 × 200 = _____

⑯ 400 × 4 = _____

UNIT 3

Solve 321 × 5

321
× 5
‾‾‾‾

Make an estimate.

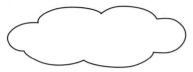

Split 321 into its place-value parts.　_____ = _____ + _____ + _____

Write three multiplication equations and add the products.

_____ × _____ = _____

_____ × _____ = _____

_____ × _____ = _____
‾‾‾‾‾‾

_____

321 × 5 = _____

Is your product close to your estimate? _____

Explain how splitting 321 into its place-value parts helped you find the product.

_____

_____

Make Estimates to Check Products

DIRECTIONS

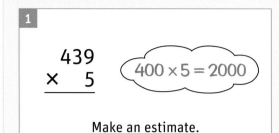

1

$$439$$
$$\times \quad 5$$

$400 \times 5 = 2000$

Make an estimate.

2

$400 \times 5 = 2000$
$30 \times 5 = \quad 150$
$9 \times 5 = \quad \underline{\quad 45}$
$\qquad\qquad 2195$

Multiply and add.

3

✓

Write a check mark if your answer is close to your estimate.

Make an estimate		Multiply and add	Check estimate
① 278 × 8			
② 781 × 3			
③ 864 × 5			
④ 614 × 9			
⑤ 583 × 6			

UNIT 3

Split Both Factors to Multiply

DIRECTIONS

➤ **Use the number-splitting strategy to find each product.**

1

$$\begin{array}{r} 34 \\ \times\ 45 \\ \end{array}$$

$30 \times 50 = 1500$

Make an estimate.

2

$$\begin{array}{r} 34 \\ \times\ 45 \\ \end{array}$$

30×45 — $30 \times 40 = 1200$
$\ 30 \times\ \ 5 = \ \ 150$
4×45 — $4 \times 40 = \ \ 160$
$\ 4 \times\ \ 5 = \ \ \ \ 20$
1530

Split both factors. Multiply. Add.

3

✓

Write a check mark
if your answer
is reasonable.

UNIT 3

①

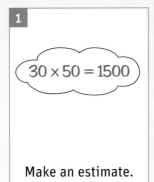

$$\begin{array}{r} 29 \\ \times\ 38 \\ \end{array}$$

②

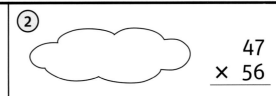

$$\begin{array}{r} 47 \\ \times\ 56 \\ \end{array}$$

③

$$\begin{array}{r} 65 \\ \times\ 74 \\ \end{array}$$

④

$$\begin{array}{r} 83 \\ \times\ 92 \\ \end{array}$$

Record Fewer Steps

23
× 48

1

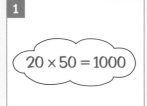

$20 \times 50 = 1000$

Make an estimate.

2

23
× 48
$20 \times 40 = 800$
$20 \times 8 = 160$
$3 \times 40 = 120$
$3 \times 8 = 24$
1104

Split both factors. Multiply. Add.

3

✓

Write a check mark
if your answer
is reasonable.

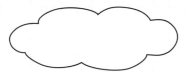

58
× 24

Explain how you made your estimate.

_____

_____

Record Fewer Steps

$$\begin{array}{r} 23 \\ \times\ 48 \end{array}$$

1

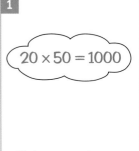

$20 \times 50 = 1000$

Make an estimate.

2

$$\begin{array}{r} 23 \\ \times\ 48 \\ \hline \end{array}$$

$20 \times 40 = 800$
$20 \times\ \ 8 = 160$
$\ \ 3 \times 40 = 120$
$\ \ 3 \times\ \ 8 = \ \underline{\ \ 24}$
$\hspace{3.5em} 1104$

Split both factors. Multiply. Add.

3

✓

Write a check mark
if your answer
is reasonable.

UNIT 3

1

$$\begin{array}{r} 33 \\ \times\ 98 \\ \hline \end{array}$$

2

$$\begin{array}{r} 66 \\ \times\ 74 \\ \hline \end{array}$$

3

$$\begin{array}{r} 25 \\ \times\ 59 \\ \hline \end{array}$$

4

$$\begin{array}{r} 85 \\ \times\ 42 \\ \hline \end{array}$$

Show What You Know

➤ Write each product.

① $3 \times 5 \times 2 =$ _____

② $200 \times 4 =$ _____

③ $2 \times 9 \times 5 =$ _____

④ $100 \times 32 =$ _____

⑤ $40 \times 6 =$ _____

⑥ $8 \times 300 =$ _____

⑦ $60 \times 80 =$ _____

⑧ $500 \times 8 =$ _____

⑨ $10 \times 29 =$ _____

⑩ $700 \times 6 =$ _____

⑪ $50 \times 70 =$ _____

⑫ $7 \times 300 =$ _____

➤ Make an estimate and then multiply.

⑬
$$\begin{array}{r} 396 \\ \times\ \ 3 \\ \hline \end{array}$$

⑭
$$\begin{array}{r} 614 \\ \times\ \ 6 \\ \hline \end{array}$$

⑮
$$\begin{array}{r} 284 \\ \times\ \ 7 \\ \hline \end{array}$$

⑯
$$\begin{array}{r} 792 \\ \times\ \ 4 \\ \hline \end{array}$$

⑰
21
× 36

⑱
89
× 50

⑲
78
× 32

⑳
19
× 43

㉑
67
× 91

㉒
33
× 29

㉓
90
× 74

㉔
88
× 39

UNIT 3

Game Rules for Product Roll

What you need

- number cube (yellow, 0–5)
- number cube (white, 4–9)
- *WorkSpace* pages 117 and 118

➤ **Each player follows the steps shown.**

1

Roll each number cube twice and record the numbers.

2

Arrange the numbers and estimate the products.

543	541	531	431
× 1	× 3	× 4	× 5

Estimates:

$500 \times 1 = 500$ $500 \times 3 = 1500$ $500 \times 4 = 2000$ $400 \times 5 = 2000$

3

Choose the problem you think has the greatest product.
Use splitting to find the product.

$$
\begin{array}{r}
4 \quad 3 \quad 1 \\
\times \qquad 5 \\
\hline
\end{array}
$$

$400 \times 5 = 2000$
$30 \times 5 = \quad 150$
$1 \times 5 = \qquad 5$
$\overline{\qquad\qquad 2155}$

4

Check your partner's work. The player with
the greater product draws a star next to it.

➤ **The winner is the player whose product is greater.**

Product Roll

DIRECTIONS

➤ Record your work.

➤ Check your partner's work.

Numbers rolled   ____   ____   ____   ____

Possible problems   ✕ ____   ✕ ____   ✕ ____   ✕ ____

Estimates   _____   _____   _____   _____

Multiplication problem   ____ ____ ____

            ✕   ____

        _____ =

        _____ =

        _____ = _____

UNIT 3

Product Roll

➤ Record your work.

➤ Check your partner's work.

Numbers rolled   _____   _____   _____   _____

Possible problems   ✕ _____   ✕ _____   ✕ _____   ✕ _____

Estimates   _____   _____   _____   _____

Multiplication problem   ____ ____ ____

           ✕ _____ ____

     _____ =

     _____ =

     _____ = _____

UNIT 3

Relay Teams With 24 Students

DIRECTIONS

1

There are 24 students.

Each relay team has 3 students.

How many teams will they have? _____

Read the problem.

2

$24 \div 3 = \underline{8}$

$\underline{8} \times 3 = 24$

How many teams will they have? __8__

Write equations.
Answer the question.

3

Check your answer with tiles.

Problem	Equations
① There are 24 students. Each relay team has 4 students. How many teams will they have? _____	
② There are 24 students. Each relay team has 12 students. How many teams will they have? _____	
③ There are 24 students. Each relay team has 8 students. How many teams will they have? _____	
④ There are 24 students. Each relay team has 2 students. How many teams will they have? _____	

UNIT 4

Relay Team Problems

1

There are 21 students.

Each relay team has 3 students.

How many teams will they have? _____

Read the problem.

2

$$21 \div 3 = \underline{7}$$
$$\underline{7} \times 3 = 21$$

How many teams will they have? ___7___

Write equations.
Answer the question.

3

Check your answer with tiles.

Problem	Equations
① There are 18 students. Each relay team has 6 students. How many teams will they have? _____	
② There are 30 students. Each relay team has 5 students. How many teams will they have? _____	
③ There are 15 students. Each relay team has 3 students. How many teams will they have? _____	
④ There are 12 students. Each relay team has 6 students. How many teams will they have? _____	
⑤ There are 25 students. Each relay team has 5 students. How many teams will they have? _____	

UNIT 4

Relay Team Problems

1 There are 21 students.
Each team has 4 students.

Can they make teams with no one left out? _____

How many teams will they have?

_____

How many are left out? _____

Read the problem and questions.

2

$21 \div 4 =$ ___5 R1___

$5 \times 4 = 20$

$6 \times 4 = 24$

Write the division and multiplication equations. Write the quotient.

3

Check your answer with tiles and then answer the questions.

Problem	Equations
1 There are 24 students. Each team has 10 students. Can they make teams with no one left out? _____ How many teams will they have? _____ How many are left out? _____	
2 There are 18 students. Each team has 5 students. Can they make teams with no one left out? _____ How many teams will they have? _____ How many are left out? _____	
3 There are 25 students. Each team has 7 students. Can they make teams with no one left out? _____ How many teams will they have? _____ How many are left out? _____	
4 There are 28 students. Each team has 4 students. Can they make teams with no one left out? _____ How many teams will they have? _____ How many are left out? _____	

UNIT 4

Game Rules for Division Bingo A

What you need

- number cube (red, 1–6)
- *WorkSpace* pages 124 and 126

➤ **Players take turns.**

1

| 20 |

$20 \div 4 = 5$
$5 \times 4 = 20$

On your turn, roll the number cube
and choose a number on the
Division Bingo card that is divisible
by the number on the cube.

Then write a division equation
and a multiplication equation.

2

Division Bingo

1	2	3	4	5
21	24	25	27	6
20	36	FREE SPACE	28	8
18	35	32	30	9
16	15	14	12	10

Mark an X on the number you chose.

3

Hand the cube to your partner.

➤ **The goal is to mark five boxes in a row—across, up and
down, or from corner to corner.**

Division Bingo

DIRECTIONS

1

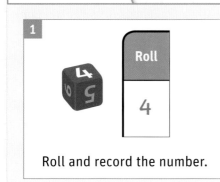

Roll
4

Roll and record the number.

2

Dividend from Bingo Card
20

Choose a dividend and record.

3

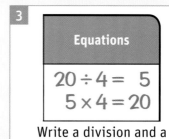

Equations

$20 \div 4 = 5$
$5 \times 4 = 20$

Write a division and a multiplication equation.

Roll	Dividend from Bingo Card	Equations

Roll	Dividend from Bingo Card	Equations

UNIT 4

Division Bingo Game Boards

A

1	2	3	4	5
21	24	25	27	6
20	36	FREE SPACE	28	8
18	35	32	30	9
16	15	14	12	10

A

1	2	3	4	5
21	24	25	27	6
20	36	FREE SPACE	28	8
18	35	32	30	9
16	15	14	12	10

A

1	2	3	4	5
21	24	25	27	6
20	36	FREE SPACE	28	8
18	35	32	30	9
16	15	14	12	10

A

1	2	3	4	5
21	24	25	27	6
20	36	FREE SPACE	28	8
18	35	32	30	9
16	15	14	12	10

Division Bingo

DIRECTIONS

1

Roll
4

Roll and record the number.

2

Dividend from Bingo Card
20

Choose a dividend and record.

3

Equations
20 ÷ 4 = 5
5 × 4 = 20

Write a division and a multiplication equation.

Roll	Dividend from Bingo Card	Equations

Roll	Dividend from Bingo Card	Equations

UNIT 4

Division Bingo Game Boards

A

1	2	3	4	5
21	24	25	27	6
20	36	FREE SPACE	28	8
18	35	32	30	9
16	15	14	12	10

A

1	2	3	4	5
21	24	25	27	6
20	36	FREE SPACE	28	8
18	35	32	30	9
16	15	14	12	10

A

1	2	3	4	5
21	24	25	27	6
20	36	FREE SPACE	28	8
18	35	32	30	9
16	15	14	12	10

A

1	2	3	4	5
21	24	25	27	6
20	36	FREE SPACE	28	8
18	35	32	30	9
16	15	14	12	10

Show What You Know

DIRECTIONS

➤ Write the division problem.
➤ Write the multiplication equation or equations.
➤ Fill in the answers.

Problem	Equations
(1) There are 27 students. Each team has 9 students. Can they make teams with no one left out? _____ How many teams will they have? _____ How many are left out? _____	
(2) There are 18 students. Each team has 4 students. Can they make teams with no one left out? _____ How many teams will they have? _____ How many are left out? _____	
(3) There are 30 students. Each team has 7 students. Can they make teams with no one left out? _____ How many teams will they have? _____ How many are left out? _____	
(4) There are 29 students. Each team has 5 students. Can they make teams with no one left out? _____ How many teams will they have? _____ How many are left out? _____	

UNIT 4

➤ For each roll, choose a dividend and record.

➤ Write a division and a multiplication equation.

➤ Mark the dividend with an X.

Division Bingo

1	2	3	4	5
21	24	25	27	6
20	36	FREE SPACE	28	8
18	35	32	30	9
16	15	14	12	10

Roll	Dividend from Bingo Card	Equations
⑤ 4		
⑥ 6		
⑦ 5		

UNIT 4

Division Bingo

DIRECTIONS

1

Roll
4

Roll and record the number.

2

Dividend from Bingo Card
20

Choose a dividend and record.

3

Equations
$20 \div 4 = 5$ $5 \times 4 = 20$

Write a division and a multiplication equation.

Roll	Dividend from Bingo Card	Equations

Roll	Dividend from Bingo Card	Equations

UNIT 4

Division Bingo Game Boards

A

1	2	3	4	5
21	24	25	27	6
20	36	FREE SPACE	28	8
18	35	32	30	9
16	15	14	12	10

A

1	2	3	4	5
21	24	25	27	6
20	36	FREE SPACE	28	8
18	35	32	30	9
16	15	14	12	10

A

1	2	3	4	5
21	24	25	27	6
20	36	FREE SPACE	28	8
18	35	32	30	9
16	15	14	12	10

A

1	2	3	4	5
21	24	25	27	6
20	36	FREE SPACE	28	8
18	35	32	30	9
16	15	14	12	10

Divide by 2

1

$56 \div 2 =$

$56 = 50 + 6$

Split the dividend into tens and ones.

2

$50 \div 2 = 25$

$6 \div 2 = \ 3$

Divide the tens.
Divide the ones.

3

$25 + 3 = 28$

$56 \div 2 = 28$

Add the quotients.
Write the answer.

① $94 \div 2 =$

② $72 \div 2 =$

③ $48 \div 2 =$

④ $34 \div 2 =$

⑤ $46 \div 2 =$

⑥ $58 \div 2 =$

⑦ $52 \div 2 =$

⑧ $96 \div 2 =$

UNIT 4

Divide by 5

1

$$85 \div 5 =$$
$$85 = 50 + 35$$

Split the dividend.

2

$$50 \div 5 = 10$$
$$35 \div 5 = 7$$

Divide the two addends.

3

$$10 + 7 = 17$$
$$85 \div 5 = 17$$

Add the quotients.
Write the answer.

---

① $75 \div 5 =$

② $70 \div 5 =$

③ $80 \div 5 =$

④ $85 \div 5 =$

⑤ $65 \div 5 =$

⑥ $90 \div 5 =$

⑦ $95 \div 5 =$

⑧ $60 \div 5 =$

UNIT 4

Divide by 10

➤ Write the answer for the division problems.

① $75 \div 10 =$	② $89 \div 10 =$
③ $67 \div 10 =$	④ $58 \div 10 =$
⑤ $95 \div 10 =$	⑥ $64 \div 10 =$
⑦ $72 \div 10 =$	⑧ $60 \div 10 =$
⑨ $91 \div 10 =$	⑩ $80 \div 10 =$

UNIT 4

Show What You Know

➤ Write the answer.

➤ If you use splitting, write the equations to show how you solved the problem.

① $96 \div 2 =$

② $69 \div 10 =$

③ $85 \div 5 =$

④ $65 \div 5 =$

⑤ $78 \div 10 =$

⑥ $84 \div 10 =$

⑦ $72 \div 2 =$

⑧ $54 \div 2 =$

⑨ $90 \div 5 =$

⑩ $90 \div 10 =$

Division Bingo

DIRECTIONS

1

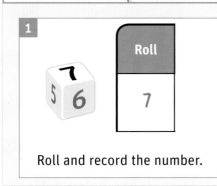

Roll
7

Roll and record the number.

2

Dividend from Bingo Card
49

Choose a dividend and record.

3

Equations
$49 \div 7 = 7$
$7 \times 7 = 49$

Write a division and a multiplication equation.

Roll	Dividend from Bingo Card	Equations

Roll	Dividend from Bingo Card	Equations

Division Bingo Game Boards

B

25	48	35
54	40	45
63	72	42

C

40	30	56
49	72	45
48	35	63

D

56	42	36
40	54	81
64	30	48

E

16	24	28	32	40
36	42	48	49	54
56	60	FREE SPACE	63	64
70	72	80	81	90
100	36	60	24	24

Division Bingo

DIRECTIONS

1		2		3	

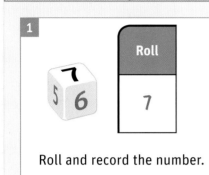

Roll
7

Roll and record the number.

Dividend from Bingo Card
35

Choose a dividend and record.

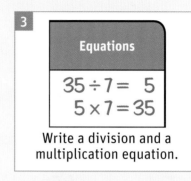

Equations
$35 \div 7 = 5$
$5 \times 7 = 35$

Write a division and a multiplication equation.

Roll	Dividend from Bingo Card	Equations

Roll	Dividend from Bingo Card	Equations

UNIT 4

Division Bingo Game Boards

B

25	48	35
54	40	45
63	72	42

C

40	30	56
49	72	45
48	35	63

D

56	42	36
40	54	81
64	30	48

E

16	24	28	32	40
36	42	48	49	54
56	60	FREE SPACE	63	64
70	72	80	81	90
100	36	60	24	24

UNIT 4

Solve Relay Problems

DIRECTIONS

1	2	3	4
There are 20 students. Each team has 4 students. How many teams can they make? Read the word problem.	$4\overline{)20}$ Write the problem. Solve with tiles if you want.	$\begin{array}{r} 5 \\ 4\overline{)20} \\ \underline{20} \\ 0 \end{array}$ $5 \times 4 = 20$ Solve with long division.	Can they make teams with no one left out? __yes__ How many teams can they make? __5__ Answer the questions.

---

① There are 30 students.
Each team has
6 students.

How many teams
can they make?

| | Can they make teams with no one left out? _____ |
| How many teams can they make? _____ |

---

② There are 32 students.
Each team has
8 students.

How many teams
can they make?

Can they make teams with no one left out? _____

How many teams can they make? _____

---

③ There are 28 students.
Each team has
4 students.

How many teams
can they make?

Can they make teams with no one left out? _____

How many teams can they make? _____

---

④ There are 35 students.
Each team has
5 students.

How many teams
can they make?

Can they make teams with no one left out? _____

How many teams can they make? _____

UNIT 4

Solve More Relay Problems

DIRECTIONS

1

There are 23 students. Each team has 4 students.

How many teams can they make?

Read the word problem.

2

$$4\overline{)23}$$

Write the problem. Solve with tiles if you want.

3

$$\begin{array}{r} 5\,R3 \\ 4\overline{)23} \\ 20 \\ \hline 3 \end{array} \quad 5 \times 4 = 20$$

Solve with long division.

4

Can they make teams with no one left out? ___no___

How many teams can they make? ___5___

Answer the questions.

---

(1) There are 28 students. Each team has 5 students.

How many teams can they make?

Can they make teams with no one left out? _____

How many teams can they make? _____

---

(2) There are 34 students. Each team has 4 students.

How many teams can they make?

Can they make teams with no one left out? _____

How many teams can they make? _____

---

(3) There are 20 students. Each team has 6 students.

How many teams can they make?

Can they make teams with no one left out? _____

How many teams can they make? _____

---

(4) There are 30 students. Each team has 7 students.

How many teams can they make?

Can they make teams with no one left out? _____

How many teams can they make? _____

Long Division Practice

$4\overline{)52}$

1

$$\begin{array}{r} 10 \\ 4\overline{)52} \\ 40 \\ \hline 12 \end{array}$$ $10 \times 4 = 40$

Write a multiplication equation.

2

$$\begin{array}{r} 3 \\ 10 \end{array} \Big\rangle 13$$

$$\begin{array}{r} 4\overline{)52} \\ 40 \\ \hline 12 \\ 12 \\ \hline 0 \end{array}$$ $10 \times 4 = 40$

$3 \times 4 = 12$

Write the division.

3

$$\begin{array}{r} 13 \\ \times 4 \\ \hline 52 \end{array}$$

Check the answer.

$4\overline{)61}$

Explain how you used multiplication to solve a long division problem.

_____

_____

_____

_____

UNIT 4

More Long Division Practice

1

$3\overline{)47}$

$$\begin{array}{r} 10 \\ 3\overline{)47} \\ 30 \\ \hline 17 \end{array} \quad 10 \times 3 = 30$$

Write a multiplication equation.

2

$$\begin{array}{r} 5 \\ 10 \\ \end{array} \Big> 15\,R2$$

$$\begin{array}{r} 3\overline{)47} \\ 30 \\ \hline 17 \\ 15 \\ \hline 2 \end{array} \quad \begin{array}{l} 10 \times 3 = 30 \\ \\ 5 \times 3 = 15 \end{array}$$

Write the division.

3

$$\begin{array}{r} 15 \\ \times 3 \\ \hline 45 \\ +2 \\ \hline 47 \end{array}$$

Check the answers.

①

$5\overline{)65}$

②

$3\overline{)54}$

③

$6\overline{)75}$

④

$4\overline{)68}$

⑤

$6\overline{)84}$

⑥

$5\overline{)57}$

Number Cube Problems

$34 \div 5 = 6$ R4

$35 \div 4 = 8$ R3

$45 \div 3 = 15$ R0

$43 \div 5 = 8$ R3

$54 \div 3 = 18$ R0

$53 \div 4 =$ _____

DIRECTIONS

➤ Solve and fill in the blank above.

$$4\overline{)53}$$

UNIT 4

Game Rules for Remainder Zero

DIVISION GAME

What you need

- number cubes (red, 1–6)
- *WorkSpace* page 145

➤ **One team plays against another team.**

1

Roll the number cube three times and record the numbers. If any numbers are the same, roll a cube again until you have three different numbers.

2

$34 \div 2$
$32 \div 4$
$24 \div 3$
$23 \div 4$
$42 \div 3$
$43 \div 2$

Write 6 problems.

3

$34 \div 2 = 17 \text{ R}0$
$32 \div 4 = 8 \text{ R}0$
$24 \div 3 = 8 \text{ R}0$
$23 \div 4 = 5 \text{ R}3$
$42 \div 3 = 14 \text{ R}0$
$43 \div 2 = 21 \text{ R}1$

Solve each problem.

4

4

Record your number of zero remainders.

➤ **The team with the greater number of zero remainders wins.**

Remainder Zero

1

Roll the number cube three times and record the numbers.

2

If any numbers are the same, roll a cube again. You need three different numbers.

3

$34 \div 5 = 6\,R4$
$43 \div 5 = 8\,R3$
$53 \div 4 = 13\,R1$
$54 \div 3 = 18\,R0$
$45 \div 3 = 15\,R0$
$35 \div 4 = 8\,R3$

Write six division problems. Solve them.

4

Number of zero remainders $\boxed{2}$

Record the number of zero remainders you have.

Numbers

Write six problems and solve. Use space below to solve.

① _____

② _____

③ _____

④ _____

⑤ _____

⑥ _____

Number of zero remainders ☐

Solve here.

Remainder Zero

1

Roll the number cube three times and record the numbers.

2

If any numbers are the same, roll a cube again. You need three different numbers.

3
$34 \div 5 = 6\,R4$
$43 \div 5 = 8\,R3$
$53 \div 4 = 13\,R1$
$54 \div 3 = 18\,R0$
$45 \div 3 = 15\,R0$
$35 \div 4 = 8\,R3$
Write six division problems. Solve them.

4
Number of zero remainders $\boxed{2}$

Record the number of zero remainders you have.

Numbers

Write six problems and solve. Use space below to solve.

(1) _____

(2) _____

(3) _____

(4) _____

(5) _____

(6) _____

Number of zero remainders ☐

Solve here.

Show What You Know

➤ Solve and check answers.

1

$$7\overline{)45}$$

2

$$5\overline{)79}$$

3

$$6\overline{)72}$$

4

$$3\overline{)57}$$

5

$$4\overline{)70}$$

6

$$6\overline{)85}$$

Division Bingo

DIRECTIONS

1

Roll
7

Roll and record the number.

2

Dividend from Bingo Card
49

Choose a dividend and record.

3

Equations
$49 \div 7 = 7$ $7 \times 7 = 49$

Write a division and a multiplication equation.

Roll	Dividend from Bingo Card	Equations

Roll	Dividend from Bingo Card	Equations

Division Bingo Game Boards

B

25	48	35
54	40	45
63	72	42

C

40	30	56
49	72	45
48	35	63

D

56	42	36
40	54	81
64	30	48

E

16	24	28	32	40
36	42	48	49	54
56	60	FREE SPACE	63	64
70	72	80	81	90
100	36	60	24	24

UNIT 4

Division Bingo

DIRECTIONS

1

Roll
5

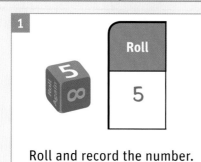

Roll and record the number.

2

Dividend from Bingo Card
30

Choose a dividend and record.

3

Equations
$30 \div 5 = 6$ $6 \times 5 = 30$

Write a division and a multiplication equation.

Roll	Dividend from Bingo Card	Equations	Roll	Dividend from Bingo Card	Equations

UNIT 4

Division Bingo Game Boards

B

25	48	35
54	40	45
63	72	42

C

40	30	56
49	72	45
48	35	63

D

56	42	36
40	54	81
64	30	48

E

16	24	28	32	40
36	42	48	49	54
56	60	FREE SPACE	63	64
70	72	80	81	90
100	36	60	24	24

UNIT 4

Scooter Problems

Heather brings 43 wheels.

How many scooters can we put together? _____

How many wheels will be left over? _____

1

$$\begin{array}{r} 4 \\ 10 \end{array} \!\!\!\!\! \Big\rangle\, 14\ R1$$

$$3\overline{)43}$$
$$\underline{30} \qquad \textcircled{10} \times 3 = 30$$
$$13$$
$$\underline{12} \qquad \textcircled{4} \times 3 = 12$$
$$1$$

Write the division problem and solve it.

2

$$14 \times 3 = 42$$
$$42 + 1 = 43$$

Check your answer.

3

How many scooters can we put together? _14_

How many wheels will be left over? _1_

Answer the questions.

Problem	Solve	Check
1 Heather brings 34 wheels. How many scooters can we put together? _____ How many wheels will be left over? _____		
2 Heather brings 49 wheels. How many scooters can we put together? _____ How many wheels will be left over? _____		
3 Heather brings 45 wheels. How many scooters can we put together? _____ How many wheels will be left over? _____		

UNIT 5

Scooter Problems

DIRECTIONS

Heather brings 74 wheels.

How many scooters can we put together? _____

How many wheels will be left over? _____

1

$$\begin{array}{r} 4 \\ 10 \\ 10 \\ 3\overline{)74} \\ \underline{30} \quad \textcircled{10} \times 3 = 30 \\ 44 \\ \underline{30} \quad \textcircled{10} \times 3 = 30 \\ 14 \\ \underline{12} \quad \textcircled{4} \times 3 = 12 \\ 2 \end{array}$$

10 ➔ 24 R2

Write the division problem and solve it.

2

$24 \times 3 = 72$

$72 + 2 = 74$

Check your answer.

3

How many scooters can we put together? __24__

How many wheels will be left over? __2__

Answer the questions.

Problem	Solve	Check
① Heather brings 81 wheels. How many scooters can we put together? _____ How many wheels will be left over? _____		

UNIT 5

Scooter Problems

DIRECTIONS

Heather brings 74 wheels.

How many scooters can we put together? _____

How many wheels will be left over? _____

1

$$
\begin{array}{r}
4 \\
10 \\
10 \\
\hline
3\overline{)74} \\
30 \\
\hline
44 \\
30 \\
\hline
14 \\
12 \\
\hline
2
\end{array}
$$

24 R2

⑩ × 3 = 30

⑩ × 3 = 30

④ × 3 = 12

Write the division problem and solve it.

2

$24 \times 3 = 72$

$72 + 2 = 74$

Check your answer.

3

How many scooters can we put together? __24__

How many wheels will be left over? __2__

Answer the questions.

Problem	Solve	Check
(1) Heather brings 79 wheels. How many scooters can we put together? _____ How many wheels will be left over? _____		
(2) Heather brings 73 wheels. How many scooters can we put together? _____ How many wheels will be left over? _____		

Skateboard Problems

Heather brings 83 wheels.

How many skateboards can we put together? ____

How many wheels will be left over? _____

1

$$10$$
$$10 \!\!> 20 \text{ R}3$$
$$4)\overline{83}$$
$$\underline{40} \quad \textcircled{10} \times 4 = 40$$
$$43$$
$$\underline{40} \quad \textcircled{10} \times 4 = 40$$
$$3$$

Write the division problem and solve it.

2

$$20 \times 4 = 80$$
$$80 + 3 = 83$$

Check your answer.

3

How many skateboards can we put together? __20__

How many wheels will be left over? __3__

Answer the question.

Problem	Solve	Check
① Heather brings 98 wheels. How many skateboards can we put together? _____ How many wheels will be left over? _____		

Skateboard Problems

DIRECTIONS

Heather brings 83 wheels.

How many skateboards can we put together? _____

How many wheels will be left over? _____

1

$$
\begin{array}{r}
10 \\
10 \\
4\overline{)83} \\
\underline{40} \quad \textcircled{10} \times 4 = 40 \\
43 \\
\underline{40} \quad \textcircled{10} \times 4 = 40 \\
3
\end{array}
$$

10 + 10 → 20 R3

Write the division problem and solve it.

2

$20 \times 4 = 80$

$80 + 3 = 83$

Check your answer.

3

How many skateboards can we put together? __20__

How many wheels will be left over? __3__

Answer the questions.

Problem	Solve	Check
① Heather brings 93 wheels. How many skateboards can we put together? _____ How many wheels will be left over? _____		
② Heather brings 88 wheels. How many skateboards can we put together? _____ How many wheels will be left over? _____		

UNIT 5

Solve Problems With Fewer Steps

DIRECTIONS

Heather brings 93 wheels.

How many skateboards can we put together? ___

How many wheels will be left over? _____

1

$$
\begin{array}{r}
3 \\
20 \\
4\overline{)93} \\
80 \\
13 \\
12 \\
1
\end{array}
$$
> 23 R1

$20 \times 4 = 80$

$3 \times 4 = 12$

Write the division problem and solve it.

2

$23 \times 4 = 92$

$92 + 1 = 93$

Check your answer.

3

How many skateboards can we put together? __23__

How many wheels will be left over? __1__

Answer the questions.

Problem	Solve	Check
① Heather brings 68 wheels. Each scooter needs 3 wheels. How many scooters can we put together? _____ How many wheels will be left over? _____		
② Heather brings 47 wheels. Each bicycle needs 2 wheels. How many bicycles can we put together? _____ How many wheels will be left over? _____		

UNIT 5

Solve Problems With Fewer Steps

Heather brings 73 wheels.

How many scooters can we put together? _____

How many wheels will be left over? _____

1

$$\begin{array}{r} 4 \\ 20 \end{array} \Big\rangle\, 24\ R1$$

$3\overline{)73}$

$\underline{60}$ $\textcircled{20} \times 3 = 60$

13

$\underline{12}$ $\textcircled{4} \times 3 = 12$

1

Write the division problem and solve it.

2

$24 \times 3 = 72$

$72 + 1 = 73$

Check your answer.

3

How many scooters can we put together? __24__

How many wheels will be left over? __1__

Answer the questions.

Problem	Solve	Check
① Heather brings 82 wheels. How many scooters can we put together? _____ How many wheels will be left over? _____		
② Heather brings 58 wheels. How many bicycles can we put together? _____ How many wheels will be left over? _____		
③ Heather brings 90 wheels. How many skateboards can we put together? _____ How many wheels will be left over? _____		

UNIT 5

Show What You Know

➤ Solve each problem with division.

Problem	Solve	Check
① Sheila brings 86 wheels. How many scooters can we put together? _____ How many wheels will be left over? _____		
② Sheila brings 54 wheels. How many skateboards can we put together? _____ How many wheels will be left over? _____		
③ Sheila brings 35 wheels. How many bicycles can we put together? _____ How many wheels will be left over? _____		

UNIT 5

Problem	Solve	Check
(4) Sheila brings 70 wheels. How many scooters can we put together? _____ How many wheels will be left over? _____		
(5) Sheila brings 96 wheels. How many skateboards can we put together? _____ How many wheels will be left over? _____		
(6) Sheila brings 49 wheels. How many bicycles can we put together? _____ How many wheels will be left over? _____		

Rules for Target Zero

What you need

- number cube (red, 1–6)
- *WorkSpace* page 162 or 163

1

Player A rolls the number cube.

2

10   20   30   40   50   60   70   80   90   ~~100~~

$$1000 - 200 = 800$$

Player A multiplies the number on the cube by a multiple
of ten, crosses out the multiple of ten,
and subtracts his or her score from 1000.

3

Player A hands the cube to Player B.

4

10   20   30   40   50   60   70   ~~80~~   90   100

$$3 \times \underline{\ 80\ } = 240$$
$$1000 - 240 = 760$$

Player B takes a turn.

➤ **Players start with a score of 1000. They subtract their
amounts from each turn from their previous scores.**

➤ **The winner is the player whose score is closer to
0—without going under—after six turns.**

UNIT 5

Target Zero

➤ Record your equations and scores.

| 10 | 20 | 30 | 40 | 50 | 60 | 70 | 80 | 90 | 100 |

Number Rolled	Multiple of Ten	Equation	Score
Roll 1			
Roll 2			
Roll 3			
Roll 4			
Roll 5			
Roll 6			TOTAL

Target Zero

DIRECTIONS

➤ Record your equations and scores.

| 10 | 20 | 30 | 40 | 50 | 60 | 70 | 80 | 90 | 100 |

Number Rolled	Multiple of Ten	Equation	Score
Roll 1			
Roll 2			
Roll 3			
Roll 4			
Roll 5			
Roll 6			TOTAL

UNIT 5

Pennies Exchanged for Nickels

DIRECTIONS

There are 527 pennies.

How many nickels can they be exchanged for? _____

How many pennies are left over? _____

1

$$\begin{array}{r} 5 \\ 100 \end{array} \Big\rangle 105 \text{ R2}$$

$$5\overline{)527}$$
$$\underline{500} \quad \textcircled{100} \times 5 = 500$$
$$27$$
$$\underline{25} \quad \textcircled{5} \times 5 = 25$$
$$2$$

Write the division problem and solve it.

2

$$105 \times 5 = 525$$
$$525 + 2 = 527$$

Check your answer.

3

How many nickels can they be exchanged for? <u>105</u>

How many pennies are left over? <u>2</u>

Answer the questions.

Problem	Solve	Check
(1) There are 608 pennies. How many nickels can they be exchanged for? _____ How many pennies are left over? _____		

Pennies Exchanged for Nickels

DIRECTIONS

There are 527 pennies.

How many nickels can they be exchanged for? _____

How many pennies will be left over? _____

1

$$\begin{array}{r} 5 \\ 100 \\ \hline 5)527 \\ 500 \\ \hline 27 \\ 25 \\ \hline 2 \end{array}$$

$\rangle$ 105 R2

(100) × 5 = 500

(5) × 5 = 25

Write the division problem and solve it.

2

105 × 5 = 525

525 + 2 = 527

Check your answer.

3

How many nickels can they be exchanged for? _105_

How many pennies will be left over? _2_

Answer the questions.

Problem	Solve	Check
① There are 615 pennies. How many nickels can they be exchanged for? _____ How many pennies will be left over? _____		
② There are 634 pennies. How many nickels can they be exchanged for? _____ How many pennies will be left over? _____		

UNIT 5

Pennies Exchanged for Nickels in Fewer Steps

DIRECTIONS

There are 734 pennies.

How many nickels can they be exchanged for? _____

How many pennies will be left over? _____

1

$$
\begin{array}{r}
6 \\
40 \\
100 \\
5\overline{)734} \\
500 \\
234 \\
200 \\
34 \\
30 \\
4
\end{array}
\longrightarrow 146\ R4
$$

$\enclose{circle}{100} \times 5 = 500$

$\enclose{circle}{40} \times 5 = 200$

$\enclose{circle}{6} \times 5 = 30$

Write the division problem and solve it.

2

$146 \times 5 = 730$

$730 + 4 = 734$

Check your answer.

3

How many nickels can they be exchanged for? __146__

How many pennies will be left over? __4__

Answer the questions.

Problem	Solve	Check
① There are 743 pennies. How many nickels can they be exchanged for? _____ How many pennies will be left over? _____		

UNIT 5

Pennies Exchanged for Nickels in Fewer Steps

DIRECTIONS

There are 734 pennies.

How many nickels can they be exchanged for?

_____

How many pennies will be left over? _____

1

$$\begin{array}{r} 6 \\ 40 \\ 100 \end{array} \Big\rangle 146 \text{ R4}$$

$$5\overline{)734}$$
$$\underline{500} \quad \textcircled{100} \times 5 = 500$$
$$234$$
$$\underline{200} \quad \textcircled{40} \times 5 = 200$$
$$34$$
$$\underline{30} \quad \textcircled{6} \times 5 = 30$$
$$4$$

Write the division problem and solve it.

2

$$146 \times 5 = 730$$
$$730 + 4 = 734$$

Check your answer.

3

How many nickels can they be exchanged for? 146

How many pennies will be left over? 4

Answer the questions.

Problem	Solve	Check
(1) There are 230 pennies. How many nickels can they be exchanged for? _____ How many pennies will be left over? _____		
(2) There are 828 pennies. How many nickels can they be exchanged for? _____ How many pennies will be left over? _____		

UNIT 5

Roll and Divide

> Write all the possible three-digit numbers.

_____ _____ _____ _____ _____ _____

> Write the least possible dividend, solve the problem, and check.

6)‾‾‾‾‾‾

Explain how you would write the least number with any three digits on the number cubes.

_____

_____

_____

_____

UNIT 5

Roll and Divide

DIRECTIONS

1	2	3	4
 Roll the number cubes and record your numbers.	572 527 752 725 275 257 Write all the possible three-digit dividends.	$\begin{array}{r} 5 \\ 40 \end{array}$ 45 R5 6)275 240 (40) × 6 = 240 35 30 (5) × 6 = 30 5 Choose and write a dividend. Then solve the problem.	45 × 6 = 270 270 + 5 = 275 Check your answer.

Numbers Rolled	Possible Dividends	Solve	Check
①		3)	
②		4)	

UNIT 5

Roll and Divide

DIRECTIONS

1

Roll the number cubes and record your numbers.

2

572	527
752	725
275	257

Write all the possible three-digit dividends.

3

$$
\begin{array}{r}
5 \\
40 \quad {\Large\rangle} \ 45 \ R5 \\
6\overline{)275} \\
\underline{240} \quad \textcircled{40} \times 6 = 240 \\
35 \\
\underline{30} \quad \textcircled{5} \times 6 = \ 30 \\
5
\end{array}
$$

Choose and write a dividend. Then solve the problem.

4

$45 \times 6 = 270$

$270 + 5 = 275$

Check your answer.

Numbers Rolled	Possible Dividends	Solve	Check
①		$5\overline{)}$	
②		$6\overline{)}$	

Divide and Check

➤ Solve the problem and check your answer.

$$8\overline{)906}$$

If you were asked to make an estimate of this quotient, how would you know it must be greater than 100?

_____

_____

UNIT 5

Roll and Divide

1

Roll the number cubes and record your numbers.

2

840

804

480

408

Write all the possible three-digit dividends.

3

$$\begin{array}{r} 5 \\ 100 \\ \overline{\smash{)}840} \\ 800 \\ \overline{40} \\ 40 \\ \overline{0} \end{array} 8 \;>105$$

$(100) \times 8 = 800$

$(5) \times 8 = 40$

Choose and write a dividend. Then solve the problem.

4

$105 \times 8 = 840$

Check your answer.

Numbers Rolled	Possible Dividends	Solve	Check
①		$7)\overline{}$	
②		$9)\overline{}$	

UNIT 5

Roll and Divide

DIRECTIONS

Roll the number cubes and record your numbers.

844
448
484

Write all the possible three-digit dividends.

$$
\begin{array}{r}
5 \\
100 \\
\hline
8)844 \\
800 \quad (100) \times 8 = 800 \\
\hline
44 \\
40 \quad (5) \times 8 = 40 \\
\hline
4
\end{array}
$$

$\longrightarrow$ 105 R4

Choose and write a dividend. Then solve the problem.

$105 \times 8 = 840$

$840 + 4 = 844$

Check your answer.

Numbers Rolled	Possible Dividends	Solve	Check
(1)		$8\overline{)}$	
(2)		$9\overline{)}$	

UNIT 5

Show What You Know

➤ Solve each problem and check each answer.

Problem	Solve	Check
(1) There are 558 pennies. How many nickels can they be exchanged for? _____ How many pennies will be left over? _____		
(2) There are 610 pennies. How many nickels can they be exchanged for? _____ How many pennies will be left over? _____		
(3) There are 267 pennies. How many nickels can they be exchanged for? _____ How many pennies will be left over? _____		

Show What You Know

➤ Solve each problem and check each answer.

①

$$4\overline{)956}$$

②

$$7\overline{)652}$$

③

$$8\overline{)452}$$

④

$$6\overline{)780}$$

⑤ If you divide 723 by 6, will the quotient be greater than or less than 100? Explain how you know.

_____

_____

Target Zero

➤ Record your equations and scores.

| 10 | 20 | 30 | 40 | 50 | 60 | 70 | 80 | 90 | 100 |

Number Rolled	Multiple of Ten	Equation	Score
Roll 1			
Roll 2			
Roll 3			
Roll 4			
Roll 5			
Roll 6			TOTAL

Dividing by 10

➤ Solve each problem and check each answer.

1

$10\overline{)134}$

2

$10\overline{)732}$

3 What is the same about the dividend and the quotient when dividing by 10?

_____

_____

_____

Dividing by 10

➤ Use the pattern to solve each problem.

➤ Choose two problems, do the division, and check the answer.

① $891 \div 10 =$ _____

② $128 \div 10 =$ _____

③ $436 \div 10 =$ _____

④ $944 \div 10 =$ _____

⑤ $587 \div 10 =$ _____

⑥ $352 \div 10 =$ _____

⑦ $265 \div 10 =$ _____

⑧ $116 \div 10 =$ _____

⑨

$10\overline{)}$

⑩

$10\overline{)}$

⑪ Explain how you can divide any three-digit number by 10 in your head.

_____

_____

_____

Divide and Check

➤ Solve the problem and check your answer.

Problem	Solve
① $30\overline{)489}$	
② $40\overline{)562}$	
③ $30\overline{)485}$	

Divide and Check

1

$$50 \overline{)\, 788}$$

Look at the problem.

2

$$50 \overline{)\, 788} \quad 15 \; R38$$

```
        5
       10  ⟩ 15 R38
  50) 788
      500
      288
      250
       38
```

check: $15 \times 50 = 750$

$750 + 38 = 788$

Write the division problem,
solve it, and check the answer.

Problem	Solve
① $40 \overline{)\, 638}$	
② $30 \overline{)\, 772}$	

UNIT 5

Divide by 12

> Solve each problem and check each answer.

① $12\overline{)135}$

② $12\overline{)284}$

③ $12\overline{)890}$

④ $12\overline{)533}$

Divide by 25

DIRECTIONS

➤ Solve the problem and check your answer.

①

$25\overline{)284}$

②

$25\overline{)392}$

③

$25\overline{)639}$

④

$25\overline{)413}$

⑤ Explain what strategies you use when you divide by 25.

_____

_____

UNIT 5

Divide by 25

➤ Solve each problem and check each answer.

① $25\overline{)356}$

② $25\overline{)301}$

③ $25\overline{)613}$

④ $25\overline{)825}$

UNIT 5

Show What You Know

➤ Solve each problem and check each answer.

①

$25\overline{)368}$

②

$12\overline{)270}$

③

$12\overline{)172}$

④

$20\overline{)685}$

⑤

$25\overline{)582}$

⑥

$30\overline{)672}$

➤ Write and solve each division problem. Check each answer.

Problem	Solve and Check
⑦ A garden store sells tulip bulbs in bags of 12. The store has 725 bulbs. How many bags will be filled? _____ How many bulbs will be left over? _____	
⑧ A museum sells peanuts in bags of 25 peanuts each. The museum has 800 peanuts. How many bags can be filled? _____ How many peanuts will be left over? _____	

➤ Answer the question.

⑨ In a long division problem, how do you know when you can stop dividing?

_____

_____

➤ Solve.

⑩ $573 \div 10 =$ _____

Rules for Target 100

What you need

- number cube (yellow, 0–5)
- number cube (red, 1–6)
- number cube (white, 4–9)
- *WorkSpace* page 187

1

567

Player A rolls the number cubes
and writes a three-digit dividend.

2

10   20   30   40   50   60   70   80   90

$50\overline{)567}$

Player A chooses a divisor from the list.

3

$$\begin{array}{r} 1 \\ 10 \\ \hline 50\overline{)567} \\ 500 \\ \hline 67 \\ 50 \\ \hline 17 \end{array} \quad \begin{array}{l} \\ \\ 10 \times 50 = 500 \\ \\ 1 \times 50 = 50 \end{array}$$

> 11 (R17)

Player A divides and circles the remainder.

4

   →

Player A hands the number cubes to Player B.

➤ **Each player adds his or her remainders after taking
five turns.**

➤ **The winner is the player whose score is closer to 100
without going over.**

UNIT 5

Target 100

| 10 | 20 | 30 | 40 | 50 | 60 | 70 | 80 | 90 |

Numbers Rolled	Division	Numbers Rolled	Division
Roll 1		Roll 4	
Roll 2		Roll 5	
Roll 3		Your total (add your remainders)	
		Your partner's total	

Draw a star beside the winning score.

Target 100

| 10 | 20 | 30 | 40 | 50 | 60 | 70 | 80 | 90 |

Numbers Rolled	Division	Numbers Rolled	Division
Roll 1		Roll 4	
Roll 2		Roll 5	
Roll 3		Your total (add your remainders)	
		Your partner's total	

Draw a star beside the winning score.

Target 100

10   20   30   40   50   60   70   80   90

Numbers Rolled	Division	Numbers Rolled	Division
Roll 1		Roll 4	
Roll 2		Roll 5	
Roll 3		Your total (add your remainders)	
		Your partner's total	

Draw a star beside the winning score.

UNIT 5

Math Vocabulary

➤ Write new words and terms in the box.

➤ Write a definition, show an example, or draw a picture for each word or term in your list.

Math Vocabulary

➤ Write new words and terms in the box.

➤ Write a definition, show an example, or draw a picture for each word or term in your list.

Math Vocabulary

➤ Write new words and terms in the box.

➤ Write a definition, show an example, or draw a picture for each word or term in your list.

Math Vocabulary

> ➤ Write new words and terms in the box.
> ➤ Write a definition, show an example, or draw a picture for each word or term in your list.

Math Vocabulary

➤ Write new words and terms in the box.

➤ Write a definition, show an example, or draw a picture for each word or term in your list.

Glossary

Associative Property of Multiplication

When multiplying 3 numbers, the two factors that you multiply first are sometimes said to be grouped together. Grouping different factors to multiply first is an example of the *Associative Property of Multiplication*. To show the grouping, we use parentheses. The parentheses tell you to multiply those two factors first.

For example, to find the product for $2 \times 3 \times 4$ we can group the numbers as $(2 \times 3) \times 4$ or $2 \times (3 \times 4)$.

(2 × 3) × 4 tells us to multiply 2×3 first.

$$6 \times 4 = 24$$

2 × (3 × 4) tells us to multiply 3×4 first.

$$2 \times 12 = 24$$

Either way you get the same answer, 24.

Commutative Property of Multiplication

Changing the order of the factors does not change the product. This is called the *Commutative Property of Multiplication*. An example of this property is $3 \times 5 = 5 \times 3$.

divide

When you split a number or separate a number of objects into equal groups you use the word *divide* to describe what you are doing. For example, if you separate 12 cookies into 3 equal groups (written like this: $12 \div 3$), you divide 12 by 3.

divided by

We read $12 \div 3 = 4$ this way: *12 divided by 3 is equal to 4*. The symbol $\div$ means *divided by*.

dividend

The number being divided into equal groups is the *dividend*. In the equation $20 \div 5 = 4$, 20 is the *dividend*.

divisible

When you get a zero remainder, you can say that the *dividend* is *divisible* by the *divisor*. For example, 20 is divisible by 5 because the quotient is 4 and the remainder is zero. 23 is not divisible by 5 because there is a remainder of 3 ($23 \div 5 = 4$ R3).

division

Division is the word for what we do when we divide.

division equation

A *division equation* is a number sentence that has two sides separated by an equal sign. Both sides have the same value and there is a division on one or both sides. Examples of *division equations* are $24 \div 6 = 4$ and $5 = 15 \div 3$.

divisor

The number you are dividing by is called the *divisor*. In the equation $12 \div 3 = 4$, the 3 is the *divisor*.

We can also write the division as $3\overline{)12}^{\,4}$ and $\frac{12}{3} = 4$ where 3 is the divisor. The divisor 3 tells us that we want to know how many groups of 3 are in 12.

equal

Equal means the same amount. For example, twelve is equal to three times four. The symbol for *equal* is $=$.

Glossary

equal groups

In *equal groups,* each group has the same amount. For example, if there are circles and each circle has 2 stars, then the stars are in *equal groups.*

equation

An *equation* is a number sentence that has an equal sign to show that two amounts have the same value.

For example, $24 = 6 \times 4$ and $5 + 8 = 13$ are *equations.*

estimate (noun)

When you answer the question *"About what will the answer be?"* you make an estimate. An estimate is something you do quickly in your head so that you have an idea about what the exact answer should be close to.

For example, to make an estimate of 57×8 you can think $60 \times 8 = 480$ so 480 is an estimate for 57×8.

factor

Factors are numbers that you multiply to get a product. For example, 3 and 7 are *factors* in the equation $3 \times 7 = 21$.

grouping problem

A problem is a *grouping problem* when there are a number of things being put in equal groups and you want to figure out how many groups there are. We can use division to solve a grouping problem.

An example of a *grouping problem* is:

  There are 24 students. (number to begin with)
  Each relay team will have 6 students. (equal groups)
  How many relay teams will they make? (number of groups)

$24 \div 6 = 4$, so there are 4 teams.

multiple

Multiples of a number are numbers that you get when multiplying that number by 1, 2, 3, 4, 5, and so on. For example, *multiples* of 5 are 5, 10, 15, 20, 25, because $5 \times 1 = 5$, $5 \times 2 = 10$, $5 \times 3 = 15$, $5 \times 4 = 20$, $5 \times 5 = 25$.

multiple of 10

Numbers that have a factor of 10 are called *multiples of 10.* They always end in zero. 10, 20, 30, 40, 50, . . . are examples of *multiples of 10.*

multiplication

Multiplication is what you do when you figure the total number of items in equal groups.

multiplication equation

A *multiplication equation* is a number sentence with an equal sign and a times sign. What is on the left side of the equal sign equals what is on the right side.

Examples of *multiplication equations* are $18 = 6 \times 3$ and $6 \times 3 = 18$.

Multiplication Property of One

The product of any number and 1 is the number. For example, 7×1 and 1×7 both equal 7.

multiply

When you multiply, you find the product of factors or the total number of items in equal groups. For example, if you multiply 5 and 2, you get the product 10.

product

A *product* is the answer you get when you multiply. For example, 21 is the *product* in the equation $3 \times 7 = 21$.

quotient

A *quotient* is the answer to the question, How many equal groups of _____ are in _____? For example, *How many groups of 2 are in 25?* or *What is 25 divided by 2?* The answer is 12. There are 12 groups of 2 in 25 so 12 is the *quotient*.

remainder

When we divide a number by another number, we are finding the number of equal groups. Sometimes there are leftovers because there aren't enough to make another group.

For example, $8 \div 3$ means *How many equal groups of 3 are in 8?*

○○○   ○○○   ○○

Dividing 8 into groups of 3 gives us 2 groups of 3 with 2 left over. The 2 is the *remainder*.

We write it this way: $8 \div 3 = 2$ R2

sharing problem

A problem is a *sharing problem* when there are a number of things being shared equally and you want to find out how many will be in each group.

An example of a *sharing problem* is:

There are 12 marbles. (number to begin with)

3 friends are going to share them. (number who will share)

How many marbles will each one get? (how many in each group)

We write it this way: $12 \div 3 =$ _____. Each friend will get 4 marbles.

square number

A *square number* is the product of a number times itself. You can show that a number is a square number if you can take that number of tiles and form a square.

For example, 16 is a *square number* because it is the product of 4×4 and you can form a square with 16 tiles.

GLOSSARY

Glossary

symbols

You use *symbols* in mathematics to name numbers $\left(12, 308, \frac{1}{2}\right)$, operations $(+, -, \times, \div)$, and relationships between numbers $(=, >, <)$.

symbols for division

$\div$ means *is divided by*.

$\frac{12}{3}$ The fraction bar is a division symbol. This means 12 divided by 3.

$3\overline{)12}$ The partial box around the 12 tells us that 12 is to be divided by 3. The quotient is written on the line above the 12.

$$3\overline{)12}^{\,4} \qquad \text{divisor}\overline{)\text{dividend}}^{\,\text{quotient}}$$

times

The word *times* means multiply. Four times two means you should combine four groups of two. The symbol for *times* is $\times$.

Zero Property of Multiplication

The product of any number and zero is zero. For example, 0×7 and 7×0 both equal 0.